Everything Old is New Again

Renee W. Stein C.M.

Unless otherwise noted, Scriptures quotations are taken from The Holy Bible, King James Version, public domain.

Scripture quotations marked (NIV) are taken from the Holy Bible, New International Version®, NIV®. Copyright © 1973, 1978, 1984, 2011 by Biblica, Inc.™ Used by permission of Zondervan. All rights reserved worldwide. www.zondervan.com The "NIV" and "New International Version" are trademarks registered in the United States Patent and Trademark Office by Biblica, Inc.™

Everything Old is New Again Copyright © 2011 © 2013
by Renee Stein C.M.
Edited by Sarah Hawkes Valente
Cover photo by Sarah Shatkin Rosales
WHATEVER IS LOVELY PUBLICATIONS
P.O. Box 34
Eagle Nest, NM
87718
All rights reserved.

To my children.

Table of Contents

Foreword, 7

Author's Preface, 10

Intro, 24

Chapter One: Before You Were Born, 26

Chapter Two: The Beginning, 28

Chapter Three: His Plan, 31

Chapter Four: A Wedding, 35

Chapter Five: Thinking like a Hebrew, 45

Chapter Six: Shabbat, 60

Chapter Seven: The Feasts of the L-rd, 65

Chapter Eight: Two Topics, 69

Chapter Nine: Everything Old is New Again, 73

Chapter Ten: The Midwives and Moses, 76

Chapter Eleven: the Big Picture, 81

Chapter Twelve: Passover, 83

Chapter Thirteen: Feast of Unleavened Bread, 86

Chapter Fourteen: Feast of First Fruits, 88

Chapter Fifteen: Shavuot, 91

Chapter Sixteen: Feast of Trumpets, 94

Chapter Seventeen: Yom Kippur, 97

Chapter Eighteen: Feast of Tabernacles, 101

Chapter Nineteen: Chanukah, 104

Chart of Preborn Journey and The Feasts, 110

Chapter Twenty: A Third Journey, 112

Chart of Feasts and the Journey of the Bride, 116

Conclusion, 118

Study References, 119

Foreword

Long before I was a writer of anything more than high school poetry, before I was a mommy blogger—before I was a mommy—before marriage, before I'd ever lived with anyone but *Mom and Dad*, I met the Steins. I'd had my heart broken in the way most nineteen years olds do; but to me, my world had ended. I put college on hold to grieve, and then I grieved to the best of my ability. *"Why doesn't she learn how to deliver babies?"* suggested sympathetic and newly pregnant friends of my parents. *"We'll pay for the schooling!" they added.* That sounded as good to me as anything else, so we loaded up the car to meet the midwife and check out the home I'd be living in just a few weeks later.

The day I moved in, I arrived just in time for a family party. Renee wasted no time in sending me to the store with her oldest son who'd come to the party without his girlfriend in tow. I later joked with one of her daughters that a Jewish "Welcome to the family!" read a lot like, "You're welcome to marry into my family!" As it turned out, though, marrying into the Stein family was not the only way to join it. Within weeks, I'd earned the title of *sister* and *daughter*, and I hold those titles proudly today.

For years now, whenever I've thought of Renee, I've pictured her lighting the Sabbath candles and reciting elegant Hebrew prayers; there is something so precious in those memories. I didn't understand what she was doing except that it was *something Jewish*, but it was something that made me want to be

Jewish, too. I can still feel the hot Colorado sun on my back as memory takes me to those lazy Saturday afternoons—walking the long fence line around her beautiful yard and glorying in the wonder of His creation. Those days were mystically peaceful. It's the same feeling I get today when I celebrate the weekly Sabbath with my children.

Life gets in the way, and it's been years since I've sat down to share a meal with the Steins. Still, we are family; and we are connected. So when Renee's daughter wrote me and insisted the Father wanted *me* to edit and publish her mother's book, I responded, "Of course! That's what family is for!" Little did I know how clearly she had heard from Him and how perfectly this book would fit into and spur on my personal exploration into the deep Hebrew roots of my faith.

When I read through the first draft of Renee's book, my mouth gaped at so many passages. The Feasts of Israel were what I had been drawn to—as if they were calling to me from the deep. Had I really experienced all of these feasts as an unborn baby just as Renee was suggesting? Could that be, just possibly, why they seemed so real to what I was still calling my *gentile heart*? Feeling further inspired and empowered, I continued a search that has led me all the way back to the beginning. The old things have truly become new and shiny to me. I now see myself, excitedly and gratefully, as part of the nation of Israel that Yeshua came to save. A mezuzah marks my threshold, kosher meats fill my fridge, and I am looking forward to my first Passover as an observant Israelite rather than a curious Gentile. Much more than that, I am learning to worship the Father in Spirit and in Truth in a way that has set me free to love Him with everything that I am. I'm thrilled to have taken part in a book that will introduce many others to this incredible journey.

-Sarah Hawkes Valente
Author and blogger at kingdomtwindom.net

Author's Preface

The Jewish Part

In College, I became utterly and totally confused after taking classes in Comparative Religions. I was to expand my mind with Mohammed, Buddha, the 100,000 idols of India, the new thinking of existentialism...and somewhere in there, the discovery of self. None of it lined up with my thinking, and it was gnawing at my heart and soul. I grew up in a rock solid Christian Church and the Word. These new ideologies didn't seem to work in my thinking *or* in the academic atmosphere. I was supposed to stretch my intellect in new directions to find out who I was? Didn't happen. Just more confusion!

I'd heard of a rabbi who was very understanding and caring of college kids; and so after a while, I went to visit him. I thought I was simply stretching myself and my intellect, like my religion professor was teaching. I wanted to see what a rabbi had to say and find out about Judaism, the mother of all religions. *There's nothing wrong with starting at the beginning!* I even worked it out with the professor to get college credit for it.

The Rabbi

The rabbi was an adorable man. He was highly thought of in the neighborhood. He talked with me for a long while and then invited me to take classes at the synagogue to learn Hebrew and the Torah[1]. It was most intriguing. I found myself thoroughly enraptured by the Torah. I always thought those books were so hard to understand. But as I listened to this learned scholar, it was no longer a book of fearful *do and do nots, or thou shalt and thou shalt nots*, or stories of a G-d[2] who sent destruction down on sinners. The way the rabbi presented it to me, it became a love story of our Creator for His children—always calling them back into His arms.

    This was *so* much better than Comparative Religions class! This was clear-cut and precise. I already knew a great deal from my early days with believing parents and a praying grandmother, but this journey drew me deeper into the roots of my faith.

    I had studied for ten months when I met a Jewish boy named Joel, and we fell in love. In order to marry a Jewish boy, one had to convert to Judaism in an Orthodox[3] Synagogue. Rabbi Binstock was more than happy to do the job.

    I enjoyed this wonderful little man who was so knowledgeable and who would take the time and trouble to teach me. He was full of spunk with his red apple-cheeks like a cherub, white hair with long curls under a yamulka[4], and a twinkle in

---

[1] The Torah is the first five books of the Holy Scriptures—the law, the foundation of the Bible.
[2] The spellings of G-d and L-rd are not misprints. The vowel is dropped out of reverence to "The Name" which scribes of old considered too awesome to speak.
[3] following the established or traditional rules of a political or religious belief, a philosophy, or a way of life
[4] a skull cap worn on the man's head to show reverence for G-d's covering

his eye. Those sessions were precious, but I soon found out that being schooled by the Orthodox meant I had to face a very big question. I was told that at some point I would have to renounce Jesus. *Oh my!* When I thought about that, I got sick to my stomach. I knew my grandmother would turn over in her grave. As a child, my precious mother and grandma would tell stories about Jesus, and in Sunday school I learned all about Him. I dreaded that forth coming moment. *What would I do?*

I flew through the tests, both the oral and the written. I kept waiting for the rabbi to ask me to renounce Jesus, but not a word about it came. I was so anxious. He had asked me all sorts of other questions, but not that one. *Had he forgotten?* Then, he asked me if I had any questions for him. Having held the dreaded question pent up within me for so long, I nervously blurted out, "Do I have to give up Jesus, Rabbi Binstock?"

Oy vey!

There was dead and immediate silence, and he quickly looked away. A void filled the room. My stomach felt like an empty pit as I sat there thinking "What have I done?"

If a woman is in a room with an ultra-orthodox man, the door is always left open out of respect. There is no touching between unmarried males and females in the ultra-orthodox religion, either. I braced myself for his answer as he got up, walked over to the door, and gently closed it. He slowly walked over to me as if pondering his reply, and then he gently put his arm around my shoulder to comfort me. In a quiet tone, so as not to be heard outside the room, he said, "My child, you see..." He paused as if to wait for his next breath, then he continued half talking and half whispering, "You see child, He is my Messiah, too! His name is Y'shua Hameshiah. He is the Sar Shalom[5]!" Then he said, "No never, you will never deny Him!" And I cried.

I had just met the first of many Messianic Jewish Believers[6]; although, at that time, I had no idea what that meant. Against the wishes of many Christian friends and relatives, and especially my parents, I embraced Judaism at the tender age of eighteen and married a Jewish boy at the age of nineteen. My parents thought I was throwing away my life. I, on the other hand, was certain I had added to it.

What at first seemed to fly in the face of reason has now become an awesome inheritance, a culmination of both old and new. Joel's family openly accepted me and laid the foundations of the Jewish way of life for me. They lived Torah to the best of their busy American lives. They taught me to celebrate the Jewish Holidays, to make Challah[7], and to light the Sabbath Candles. To date, I have been Jewish longer than most of you reading this have been alive. Thus, you have the Jewish part.

---

[5]Prince of Peace
[6]A Jewish person that accepts Jesus as the Messiah
[7]A ceremonial bread that is for Shabbat/Sabbath

A Message Received from the L-rd

I was a high-fashion model for Saks Fifth Avenue, both in Chicago and Los Angeles in the early 1960's. Sounds pretty glitzy, and it was. Joel and I lived in Chicago for a few years after we married. Joel's father, Lee Stein, was one of Chicago's top entertainers. Newspaper man, Erv Cupsenet, would highlight Lee's playing around town in his syndicated "Cups Column". We met many famous people around Lee's piano. One was the famous actress Myrna Loy, who at the time was promoting a new Hollywood film, *From the Terrace,* with Paul Newman and Joan Woodward. She was a wonderful woman and must have been sent by an angel.

After chatting for a while, Myrna turned to us and actually spoke into our future. She simply said that we should follow our heart and G-d would make our dreams come true. Her seemingly common advice must have been the L-rd whispering in our ears to give us a needed push. I was pregnant with our first child, and Joel was so lonesome for the rest of his family in California; we needed to return to Los Angeles. With Ms. Loy's little message ringing in our ears, we packed it all up. We left Chicago in 1962, and I continued to work for Saks Fifth Avenue, in Beverly Hills, well into my fourth month of pregnancy.

Knock-em-Out

A strong influence in my life, my new Jewish aunts encouraged me to go to their doctor, the best Jewish OBGYN in town. Once there, I found I would have to kneel before the hierarchy of medicine and have our baby "their" way. My stomach knotted. You must remember, this was still the era of *"knock-em out drag-em out"* birth. Technology was on the horizon, bringing with it better and stronger drugs. And where was the father during this horrific, absent-mother birth? He was also absent, banished down the hall to the smoking rooms! I wanted no part of it!

There was only one doctor in the whole of Los Angeles—*one*—who did not believe in the use of drugs. His name was Robert A. Bradley. At this time, it was common medical belief that the drugs they were giving birthing mothers did not cross the placenta. Bradley disagreed. This solitary OBGYN pioneer also believed that G-d created women to birth without medical paraphernalia and interventions. He taught that birth was not an emergency. G-d created women to birth as a normal function of procreation. His research found that many babies needed to be resuscitated after birth due to all the drugs given to their mothers. After labor, the drugged mothers were often forced to stay flat on their backs, enduring horrific headaches until the drugs worked their way out of their systems. During this after-birth ordeal, poor baby was left in the baby concentration camp (phrase coined by the late Dr. Robert A. Bradley), i.e. the hospital nursery. Baby was bottle-fed and exposed to all manner of germs and disease without the defense of breast milk. When the mother could finally hold her baby, he was so used to being bottle-fed there was little to no hope for breastfeeding. *I wonder if the dads were still down the hall in the smoking rooms all that time?* Doctor Bradley also said that since drugs were openly used in the birthing theater which transferred to the baby, we would see a drug culture, a generation twenty years later, in those same children. Look at the kids twenty to thirty years after he said that! Amazing.

Nope, natural childbirth was for us! We attended natural childbirth classes and learned all the mechanics of each stage of labor and birth. We learned techniques of relaxation to reduce tension and eradicate fear, and Joel learned to be my birthing coach. He became well-read on how to spot tension in my body, he brought me popsicles and ice chips during labor, and we moved through one of life's most powerful and life-changing events—birthing our child together—"together" being the optimum word. We started this baby together in the intimacy of our home, and together we saw our newborn for the first time!

After the birth, a couple of hours or so, we were allowed to go home; so out the front door of the hospital we went. That was unheard of in that day! Little did we know, we were witnessing the start of the natural childbirth revolution and the birthing rooms women now enjoy today. While Joel and I began raising our little family and sharing our story, the interest in natural childbirth methods was growing. Robert A. Bradley, MD authored his book, <u>Husband-Coach Childbirth, The Bradley Method of Natural Childbirth</u> (referenced above); and a couple from Sherman Oaks, California made the method famous.

The Breech

During our third pregnancy, I was told I would need a Caesarian Section because the baby was in breech position—upside down, bottom first. I was devastated. My two previous children were born totally naturally, no drugs, no bleeding. They were my joy babies! We walked into the hospital and walked out. This news was just unbelievable to me. Hearing I needed a surgical procedure to cut my baby out; well, I thought this was the end of my world.

What does a good Jewish girl do when she's in trouble? She calls her rabbi. Hysterically, I told him the news. His reply was static, "Well, your doctor is probably right. You just do as he says." During these years, fear and lack of knowledge of childbirth left it a mystery to laymen. It belonged only to the gods of the medical field and not to lay people, not even a rabbi.

The Believer Part

Abba[8] brought into my life a darling woman named Evy. She was my neighbor and just happened to be pregnant with her seventh child, which I thought was a miracle in itself! In the sixties, the flower children were only supposed to have 2.4 children per household, one dog, and a station wagon parked somewhere in suburbia! But here she was, all smiles, always saying "Praise the L-rd!" for everything and at any given hour. Boy, could I ever use whatever it was that she had!

After telling her about my "breech" situation and how disappointed I had become, she was adamant I come with her to a ladies" group up in the mountains. She insisted that it would help uplift and encourage my heart. I knew I needed something.

---

[8] Hebrew for Father—G-d

A Mountain Top Experience

Upon arriving, the one thing that stood out to me most is that everyone there had that same beautiful "Evy smile," and they all said "Praise the L-rd" for everything, too. Such joy! After introductions, we were invited to sit on the floor, and we began to sing some songs. Among these songs were *Jesus Loves Me*, *This Little Light of Mine*, and of course, *Cum Ba Ya*! It was the sixties, remember?

The ladies shared stories of answered prayer from the week before. One had a financial miracle, another whose marriage needed repair said that her husband had come home, and one woman's son who was addicted to heroin was miraculously set free! They rousingly said many more choruses of "Praise the L-rd!" Then, they prayed and sang some more. All of this was a little foreign to me.

We broke for lunch, which miraculously showed up on the kitchen table. Somewhere in mid-bite, a rosy-cheeked grandma lovingly came over to me and asked questions about my being Jewish. She praised *what a great heritage* I had and asked how that was working out for me. But even before I had a chance to answer, wasting no time, another gal came up and asked "Have you ever invited your Jewish Messiah, Y'shua—Jesus into your heart?" Whoa! *MY* Jewish Messiah?—into my heart? At first I was startled. In defense, I rolodexed through memories of my childhood days— my parents, my grandma, Sunday school. I quickly decided to say, "Yes, of course!" But, I was lying through my teeth. What I had was a religion, not a personal relationship with the L-rd. There is an amazing difference, as I was about to find found out.

Unquestionably, I knew all *about* Him, but I had never asked Him to take over my life. In that moment, when I lied and said "yes," something broke deep inside my soul. I felt something happening on the inside of me. Peace and calm covered me like a warm blanket. The presence of G-d was in that room and all over me. When I said yes to that question, it became the truth. Right then and there, I accepted Y'shua as my L-rd, and I felt a deep and wonderful release. I felt clean and new.

Accepting Y'shua as my Messiah and my L-rd was a new concept because I had always been in the driver's seat. I called the shots. But now, they told me to ask for forgiveness and *surrender*. He would sit in the driver's seat and take the wheel of my life. He would do the driving from now on. They called it salvation, a completion of Judaism and Messiah. I was saved from sin—a pure gift prophesied in the Old Testament. I turned my life over to Hashem[9] and was restored and forgiven.

Still holding on to my half eaten sandwich, there was another question asked which caused me to swallow hard. "Had I ever been baptized in the Holy Spirit?" *Oh! Oh! Baptized? Was there a bathtub full of water waiting for me to be dunked in; a swimming pool, perhaps?* I had never heard of such a thing. It totally surprised me. Suddenly, I found myself whisked away to a chair in the middle of the room; later, I found out they called it the "Hot Seat". No wonder! They explained that The Baptism of the

---

[9] Hashem is Hebrew for "the Name of G-d".

Holy Spirit that is promised to all of us in the *Brit Hadesha*[10] in the Book of Acts. This baptism is an emersion in the power of G-d. The Book of Acts was one of my favorites. I especially loved the part about the mighty rushing wind and tongues of fire. Speaking in an unknown language, that was my favorite part! But I thought it was just a nice story in the New Testament.

Resurrection Power

The women asked permission to pray for me to receive His power, and then they lovingly laid hands on me. They even put their hands on my very pregnant, eighth month breech belly. They prayed that the birth would be easy, and that the baby, too, would be filled with the Holy Spirit.

I invited the Holy Spirit, the Ruach HaKodesh, into my life. He would be there always to lead me, guide me, and show me the power of the L-rd. When asking for the Holy Spirit—the Comforter— to come, I put my hands up to heaven to surrender to Him. I began speaking in another language! At that moment, my huge eight month sized pregnant belly rose up; I could scarcely breathe as my middle pitched violently to and fro. At the sight of this, everyone grew silent. Evy thought I was going to have that baby right then and there! Watching their faces was priceless. Suddenly, I could breathe freely again and I did not have a ball (the baby's head) pressing up under my ribcage any more. Oh, my gosh! The baby had turned!

---

[10] name of the "New Testament" in Hebrew

Hugs from the L-rd

A few weeks later, I was awakened with contractions I call "Hugs from the L-rd," and I immediately began singing in my new language. Surprisingly, the contractions were easy like pressure. But when I did not pray in tongues or stay in the Spirit, they were so uncomfortable I cried. I tried to use deep breathing which is taught in the classes, but only praying in tongues and staying in the Spirit made the difference. Singing in the Spirit became my birth song[11].

During certain times when I had to push, air I was supposed to use for pushing would involuntarily escape through my vocal cords causing what I thought was a very loud moaning noise. But others said they only heard me sing in my angel language, my birth song, all the way through those contractions. I sang out a gorgeous baby girl, no blood, no tearing, nursed her on the table, and went home. What a miracle! Remember, this was a breech situation only a few weeks before!

The Midwife Part

Now, since you have both the Jewish part and the Believer part of this story, you need the midwife part to see how this all comes together. We have to rewind again, back to Evy—the miracles continue!

---

[11] Many midwives call the escaping air through the vocal cords of a birthing mother, the Birth Song. It is totally involuntary.

Evy was just about due to have her baby when she called and asked me to come over to stay with the kids so that she could go to see her doctor. "Sure," I said. "I'll be right there." When I walked into the house, I could hear those *"Praise the L-rd's—*her birth song coming from the bedroom. I followed Evy's birth song to the bathroom—to the shower to be exact. Well, a long story short, I helped her deliver a beautiful baby boy right there in that shower. No tearing, no blood, only joy! It seemed as if I knew what to do just as it was presented to me. First, I saw the top of the head, which did look like a walnut[12] of sorts. Next, I saw a fat purple face and even found a cord around the neck—which I logically unwound. Then whoosh, the whole baby! You could see the breath of G-d blowing life into his entire body as he turned pink and began hollering for mama.

Now, you ask, "How did you know to do any of this?" That's the point! I didn't! But G-d did! It's part of those gifts of the Holy Spirit—wisdom and knowledge. He led me supernaturally, step-by-step. There was no time to be nervous or afraid. It was happening right then and there. I began hearing the Spirit of G-d, and I calmly and instantly *knew* what to do.

When Evy's husband came in, he swooped up all the children, and they all climbed into bed with mom and baby. What a picture! There she was, smiling her "Evy smile" and saying over and over, "Praise the L-rd!" as she kissed those tiny toes and fingers. I

---

[12] The plates of an infant's scull are designed to overlap to allow for the compression of the pelvis and vaginal walls. Some call it molding.

decided right then and there: this is the way every child should be welcomed to this planet! To this day, I can still feel the imprint of the baby's head in the palm of my hand.

> *Isaiah 51:16 (NIV) I have put my words in your mouth. I have kept you safe in the palm of my hand.*

This was the beginning. This was the day I knew beyond any shadow of a doubt—I was to become a midwife—G-d's midwife. And the L-rd supernaturally guided me, not only on the day Evy gave birth, but for the next four decades through nearly 2,500 births in seven countries. I call each and every one my Kingdom Babies, and I dedicate them to the L-rd on the spot. Today, I now smile the "Evy smile" and I say "Praise the L-rd" for everything. Amazing what the L-rd can do!

Intro

You received a beautifully engraved invitation to attend a long hoped for Jewish wedding, and you immediately decided to go. Across the top is scrolled a scripture from the Tenach.

"He brought me to the banqueting-house and his banner over me was love" – *Song of Solomon 2:4*

The ceremony was lavish in every way, no expense spared—and of course, all in Hebrew. The bride and groom were pronounced man and wife giving way to the reception with jubilant shouts of "L'chaim!"—Hebrew for "To life". You stand now surveying the reception hall filled with laughing guests, beautifully dressed children, soul swelling music, and glistening, immaculate table settings. Banquet tables overflow with food! You find your seat and your place card—your name has never looked so beautiful—and you happily introduce yourself to everyone around you. The guests have come from far and wide and the blend of languages only adds to the music. As you approach the banquet tables, you're struck by the thought that you will never be able to choose. "What a tremendous feast!" As you fill your plate to overflowing, you decide to try some of the delicacies with which you're unfamiliar. "What if I don't like it?" you worry. But you want to try everything that has been prepared for you; and to your delight, the something new is amazing.

As you read this book, I believe you'll find the something new just as amazing. Sit back and enjoy this feast of tradition and truth, give the Scriptures time to settle, enjoy the new, flip back through for seconds and thirds, and thoroughly enjoy the many "Yum!" moments that await you here.

Chapter One: Before You Were Born

I've spent a long time compiling what is written here, in bits and pieces piled high on the desk of a busy midwife. Through years of scriptural research, talking with expert upon expert, and spending countless hours in prayer, I have become fully convinced of a startling likeness between two events crucial to my own life.

I've been a Jewish Believer for many years, and while I first only cocked my head in interest, I eventually became overwhelmed as I watched The Feasts (given to Israel by G-d) appear in every area of my life—not least of all the pregnancy and birthing process. As I've eagerly searched and been rewarded to find, there is an amazing parallel between the journey of the Chosen People of G-d and the growth and development of a preborn[1] human child. I believe that as a Jewish midwife I was in a unique position to make these connections. It is with great excitement that I share them with you!

The Feasts are there, ever present, written in both the Torah and Western Bibles, but Westerners do not typically recognize them nor think them relevant to their system of worship today. And yet, they remain—vividly proclaimed for all mankind! They're in the secret place, likened to the life of the preborn who also dwells in the secret place. Now that the secret life of the preborn is easily seen with modern technology, can we understand just a bit more of the awesomeness of G-d.

---

1 The author's term for the unborn

In what I write here, it's my desire to express His love to you by demonstrating that He met with you in your mother's womb—that He desires to meet with you still. You celebrated every one of the Torah Feasts, just as our Messiah did, before you were even born!

That's right! When this was first presented to me, I was dumbfounded with joy! Even though we have no conscious recollection, each and every person alive has experienced all the Feasts of the Torah *before* being born! Our memories may be dim, but because our cells have memory, they do remember!

Let's now tip-toe back in time—to the Torah. We will examine closely the life of the preborn, probably do some readjusting of our thinking, and become enraptured by the wonder of G-d's creativity and power. We will think as one to whom the Scriptures were originally written; and as we do so, we will understand them like never before! It is my great hope that this path will deepen your love of Scripture as well as your relationship with the L-rd, our creator Hashem. As you begin your journey, please do so with this in mind: His banner over YOU is love.

Chapter Two: The Beginning

To start at the beginning of this story, we have to go all the way back to Genesis and the fall of man in the Garden of Eden. The antichrist spirit was in the Garden; and as we have seen, it is this spirit that has tried to eradicate the Chosen throughout *his*tory. After the incident over the forbidden fruit, both Adam and Eve suffered excruciating separation from G-d for their sin of rebellion. They were cast out of Paradise to toil and to till the land. A manufacturer's warrantee came with all of G-d's creation, but sin in any form nullifies the warrantee. If the blessings come off, the protection comes off, too! We see this in the accounts of Cain and Able, Esau and Jacob, and on and on. But even before all of this sin and separation in the earth, it had already happened in heaven.

> *Pride goeth before destruction and an haughty spirit before a fall. – Proverbs 16:18*

Pride incarnate, one narcissistic angel—before his expulsion from heaven, his name was Lucifer. He was gorgeous, talented, and in charge of all the worship and music of heaven. But he overestimated himself, became "puffed up" with pride, he arrogantly told the Most High G-d that he would sit on a high mountain and be higher than Elohim[1]!

---

[1] Hebrew term for G-d

This must have infuriated our Creator. Just as He tells us to throw out all leaven on the Feast of Passover, G-d cleaned house, too. The Most High G-d cast Lucifer and a third of the angels out of Heaven. Lucifer, having forever lost his title, was thenceforth called Satan. Satan continued to (as he still does, today) fight the Almighty by seducing the people of G-d. His desire is to deceive or kill anything that G-d has blessed or that blesses G-d, especially the Chosen of G-d.

With a third of the angels fallen, Satan sends out his agents of destruction who come to kill, to rob, and to destroy the people of G-d. There is a saying: *Our Creator, Hashem, consecrates; Satan tries to desecrate*. Nothing could be truer!

Even with the loss of a third of those created beings—fallen angels—our magnificent Creator moved forward. In essence, He said, *"It's no big deal. I will simply create a people who will sing praises unto me, the Most High G-d"*. To make it even better, He added, *"and I will inhabit those praises!"* Thus, He created mankind.

Can you imagine? The very G-d that created us inhabits our praise and thanksgiving! And when His creation, mankind, was pulled from perfection by the deceiver, He did not cast us out with permanence. No, He began to woo us back. He began, immediately, to put into effect His plan of rescue.

Satan has done everything possible to thwart that plan. Israel's history is a compilation of abuse and slavery that spans the ages because we are at war—not against flesh and blood, but against the supernatural. The spirit of antichrist has been on the earth since Adam and Eve, and it has subtly tried to desecrate the things of G-d.

We will begin our journey with G-d's covenant promise to Abraham. Later on, we will see Moses, used by Hashem, who continues the grooming of a rough-necked people into a priestly nation—the Hebrews whose name is later changed to Israel. We'll learn about the Ketubah—our marriage covenant and deed to the land. We'll study the law given to Moses, the Sh'ma, and Shabbat. And with tremendous excitement, we'll delve into those great feasts found in Leviticus twenty-three and Deuteronomy six and learn how they pertain to *you* today!

Chapter Three: His Plan

Generations after the incident in the garden, Hashem called Abraham who heard G-d and obeyed. Hashem always had a plan to redeem mankind. In Genesis, we read that Abraham was to leave his country and proceed on a path of blessing. This Ketubah was made and lived out through Abraham. We find in Genesis 12:1-3 the covenant between Abraham and Almighty G-d. It is your covenant as well. Hashem spoke to Abraham saying,

> *"Get thee out of thy country, and from thy kindred, and from thy father's house, unto a land that I will shew thee: And I will make of thee a great nation, and I will bless thee, and make thy name great; and thou shalt be a blessing: And I will bless them that bless thee, and curse him that curseth thee: and in thee shall all families of the earth be blessed."*

As the generations passed, Abraham's son Isaac bore Jacob and Jacob (whose name was changed to Israel) bore twelve sons. These chosen and blessed peoples were nomads. They were hungry, and famine was everywhere they went. They heard that Egypt was thriving, so they encamped just outside the pagan empire.

Joseph was Jacob's eleventh son; he was favored by Jacob and by G-d. Due to a painfully G-d breathed incident from his childhood, Joseph spent most of his time in Egypt. He advanced from prison to second in command to the Pharaoh. He saved his family from famine by moving them to Egypt, and all went well for several years. You can read the full account in *Genesis 44*. It's wonderful to see how G-d works. After Joseph died and his generation passed, a new pharaoh abused and oppressed the Chosen until G-d sent Moses as their rescuer. G-d called Moses to lead them out of captivity; after which, rebellion led them to the wilderness. But in the wilderness, G-d had a plan. There, G-d led both the natural born of Israel and those who had joined themselves to the covenant. He taught them integrity through the Law given to Moses on Mt. Sinai. He gave them a hope of the land promised.

> *And Moses called all Israel, and said unto them, Hear O Israel, the statutes and judgments which I speak in your ears this day, that ye may learn them and keep, and do them. – Deuteronomy 5: 1*

During the wilderness part of their journey, the Israelites were led by a cloud by day and fire by night. Manna—food from heaven—was sent in the early mornings. As simple nomads in the wilderness, they matured as a people and earned a wonderful new identity [*Genesis 32*]. On the day they received the Law, they also received a new name. Now, they had a new name and a new identity—the Bride. G-d calls Israel His wife.

For thy maker is thine husband. —Isaiah 54: 5, 6

All through Scripture, G-d is found protecting, leading, and wooing His wife, Israel. Yes, Hashem calls Himself a husband of Israel. As a Western thinker, this Scripture just blew my mind!

"For thy maker is thine husband, the L-rd of hosts is his name: and thy Redeemer the Holy One of Israel; the G-d of the whole earth shall he be called."

Jeremiah 3:14 concludes,
"I am married to you."

Scripture is clear that G-d betrothed Himself to Israel, and He calls her His wife! Though Israel and Judah[1] continuously strayed from the covenant and proved unfaithful to Him, He continued to woo them. He still calls out for His people today.

Many generations after leaving the wilderness and entering the Promised Land, a son, Y'shua, was born. Y'shua is called the Lamb of G-d [John 1]. It was this Lamb who grew in favor with Father G-d, lived a sinless life, and was sacrificed for the sins of the world. He died, resurrected, and then returned to the Father. The drawing that all mankind feels toward G-d is His wooing them to the

---

[1] The Whole House of Israel was divided into two separate kingdoms (The House of Israel and the House of Judah) in 931 B.C.

very covenant He made with Israel. This is the covenant Y'shua will return again to consummate [Jeremiah 31:31]! In Scripture, we read that the Lamb of G-d will return for His Bride to fulfill the covenant G-d made with her and take her to the heavenly wedding feast. Where are we on this journey? How long until we are feasting with the Bridegroom of Heaven?

Chapter Four: A Wedding

Let's pause for a Jewish wedding. A wedding is central to Jewish life because it reflects very deep truths between the Hebrew people and Hashem.

I recently attended a beautiful Jewish wedding. I noticed the photographer eagerly snapping pictures of the beautifully dressed wedding couple, the seated guests in their finery, and excited children chasing each other between shrills of giddy laughter. He snapped pictures of the flowers, the dance floor, the band, and many, many of the festive banquet tables.

New Beginnings

The joy of the wedding feast is one of new beginnings for the betrothed and for their honored guests. In addition to wishing the newlyweds well, this day is a renewing of marriage vows for all married guests in attendance. On a spiritual level, the sages of old teach that the marriage ceremony is a re-enactment of the marriage between G-d and His Chosen People which took place at Mount Sinai. For every Jewish person, their wedding day is a personal Yom Kippur[1]—the holiest and most awesome day in a Hebrew's life.

---

[1] Yom Kippur is the Holy Day of atonement. Leaving behind all transgressions, it is a clean slate.

The Wedding in Two Parts

From ancient times, formal Hebrew marriages have taken place in two parts. First is the betrothal, and second is the consummation and wedding feast. Between these ceremonies is a period of waiting.

In Jewish tradition, when a marriage contract, or Ketubah, is agreed upon between two families, the couple becomes formally betrothed. In modern times, the period of waiting is shorter; but in days past, the engagement was as long as a year or as long as it took the groom to prepare a home for his beloved. The bride would spend this time preparing for her special day. During her waiting period, the bride is called—above all else—to remain faithful.

I will even betroth thee unto me in faithfulness and thou shalt know the L-rd. — Hosea 2:20

Sanctification and Dedication

In traditional Hebrew literature, marriage is described as "sanctification" and "dedication" to G-d and to one another. Sanctification is a setting apart. Since the couple will not see each other between the betrothal and the wedding ceremony, the setting apart begins at the time of the betrothal. The two come back together as one—dedication—because future generations could not happen if man was alone. It takes two to procreate. When G-d had created man, He said:

> *And the L-rd G-d said, It is not good that the man should be alone; I will make him an help meet for him.* — Genesis 2:18

Dedication indicates an exclusive relationship, total devotion to each other—one soul in two bodies. For the betrothed, this dedication is a new beginning.

> *Therefore shall a man leave his father and his mother, and shall cleave unto his wife: and they shall be one flesh.* — Genesis 2:24

The Ketubah or Contract

Signing and witnessing of the *Ketubah* is a custom dating back to Biblical times. This contract details the husband's obligations to his wife: food, clothing, dwelling, and pleasure. It also creates a lien on all of his property to pay her a sum of money and support should he divorce her or predecease her. The document is signed, witnessed by two people, and is a legally binding agreement. This brings to mind another important contract from ancient times that pertains to you and me.

Remember that when G-d spoke to Abraham, He promised Abraham that his seed would number as many as the sands of the seas and stars in the heavens. He promised that his seed would be protected and guided through all time. This is our Ketubah, our contract with Almighty G-d. He promises to care for and protect His Chosen people; but we must hear and obey!

Veiling or Bedekin

There is more to understand from the wedding ceremony as we go on. The veiling of the bride, or the Bedekin, is done at the signing of the *Ketubah* which is usually accompanied by light snacks along with toasting and shouts of *"L'chaim!"* The groom does the *bedekin* or "veiling". Together with his father and future father-in-law, musicians and male guests go into a room where the groom covers the bride's face with a beautiful veil.

This ceremony is for the legal purpose of the groom identifying the bride before the wedding. Remember the story of Laban and Jacob [Genesis 29]? Learning from the misfortune of his forefathers, the bridegroom will not be fooled. Our Bridegroom will not be fooled! He knows who his Bride is. The veiling ceremony signals to the public that his beloved is now off the market; she is engaged, cared for, betrothed. Now, her job is to remain faithful. He will come for her, warning her only by the sound of a trumpet. And he will come in the middle of the night! More than likely, you are beginning to see some similarities in our relationship with the Bridegroom of Heaven.

On their wedding day, the bride is called the Kallah-Queen and the groom is called the Chosson-King. The royal couple is splendidly adorned in flowing white garments—the color of purity and righteousness (right usefulness). The bride wears her family's finest jewels and dresses herself in royal beauty.

I will greatly rejoice in the L-rd, my soul shall be joyful in my G-d; for he hath clothed me with the garments of salvation, he hath covered me with the robe of righteousness, as a bridegroom decketh himself with ornaments, and as a bride adorneth herself with her jewels. — Isaiah 61:10

Chuppah

The *Chuppah* is a beautifully decorated piece of cloth which is held aloft as a symbolic home for the new couple. This is a beautiful part of the ceremony, usually held outside under the stars as a sign of the blessing given by G-d to the patriarch, Abraham. Scripture promised that his children would be *"as the stars of the heavens"*.

The groom, wearing a white robe known as a *kittel,* is accompanied to the *Chuppah* by his parents. The kittel represents purity. For the bride and groom, married life starts with a clean slate; they become a brand new entity without any acknowledgment of past sins. The bride and groom have fasted on the day of the wedding because this is their personal *Yom Kippur* or Day of Atonement. All sin is wiped away so that the *two may become one* without leaven or sin.

When the bride comes to the *Chuppah* with her parents, a cantor sings from the Song of Songs. Arriving at the *Chuppah,* she circles the praying groom seven times with her mother and future mother-in-law. This ritual of circling is symbolic of the woman becoming the encircling light of the home, illuminating it with love from above and within. The number seven is also symbolic of the seven days of creation and emphasizes the fact that the bride and groom are about to create their own "new world" together with Hashem at their center. The process of *two becoming one* is taking place.

Blessing of the Wine

For all Hebrews, wine represents new life. Under the Chuppah, a rabbi recites a blessing over the wine—blessings of praise and thanksgiving to G-d for giving the sacred laws of purity and morality that preserve Jewish family life and the Jewish people.

All wine begins as a lowly grape. As it is pressed down, it turns into grape-juice. The juice ages and ferments becoming very sour, but in the end of the process, it has a wonderful sweetness. This sweetness brings joy. Wine, like all of life, begins lowly but ends sweetly. The full cup of wine also suggests the overflowing of divine blessings.

> *Thou preparest a table before me in the presence of mine enemies: thou anointest my head with oil; my cup runneth over. — Psalm 23:5*

After the bride and groom drink from the cup, the groom places a plain gold band on the finger of his bride. In the presence of two witnesses, he says, *"Behold you are consecrated to me with this ring, according to the ritual of Moses and Israel"*. The ring symbolizes the groom's role of encompassing, protecting, and providing for his wife just as Hashem protects and provides for His Chosen. Then, the rabbi recites seven blessings (Brachas).

Seven Blessings   Sheva Brachas

The **Sheva Brachot** (Hebrew: שבע ברכות) literally "the seven blessings" also known as *birkot Nesuim* (Hebrew: ברכות נישואים) are as follows:

Baruch Ata HaShem Elokainu Melech HaOlam, SheHakol Barah Lichvodo
Blessed are you, L-rd our G-d, the sovereign of the world, who created everything for his glory.

Baruch Ata HaShem Elokainu Melech HaOlam, Yotzer Ha'Adam
Blessed are you, L-rd our G-d, the sovereign of the world, the creator of man.

Baruch Ata HaShem Elokainu Melech HaOlam, Asher Yatzar Et Ha'Adam Betzalmo, b'Tzelem Dmut Tavnito, VeHitkon Lo Mimenu Binyan Adei Ad. Baruch Ata HaShem Yotzer Ha'Adam
Blessed are you, L-rd our G-d, the sovereign of the world, who created man in His image, in the pattern of His own likeness, and provided for the perpetuation of his kind. Blessed are you, L-rd, the creator of man.

Sos Tasis VeTagel HaAkarah, BeKibbutz Bane'ha Letocha BeSimchaa. Baruch Ata HaShem, Mesame'ach Tzion BeVaneha

Let the barren city be jubilantly happy and joyful at her joyous reunion with her children. Blessed are you, L-rd, who makes Zion rejoice with her children.

Sameach TeSamach Re'im Ahuvim, KeSamechacha Yetzircha BeGan Eden MiKedem. Baruch Ata HaShem, MeSame'ach Chatan VeKalah

Let the loving couple be very happy, just as You made Your creation happy in the garden of Eden, so long ago. Blessed are you, L-rd, who makes the bridegroom and the bride happy.

Baruch Ata HaShem Elokainu Melech HaOlam, Asher Barah Sasson VeSimcha, Chatan VeKalah, Gila Rina, Ditza VeChedva, Ahava VeAchava, VeShalom VeRe'ut. MeHera HaShem Elokeinu Yishama BeArei Yehudah U'Vchutzot Yerushalayim, Kol Sasson V'eKol Simcha, Kol Chatan V'eKol Kalah, Kol Mitzhalot Chatanim MeChupatam, U'Nearim Mimishte Neginatam. Baruch Ata HaShem MeSame'ach Chatan Im Hakalah.

Blessed are you, L-rd our G-d, the sovereign of the world, who created joy and celebration, bridegroom and bride, rejoicing, jubilation, pleasure and delight, love and brotherhood, peace and friendship. May there soon be heard, L-rd our G-d, in the cities of Judea and in the streets of Jerusalem, the sound of joy and the sound of celebration, the voice of a bridegroom and the voice of a bride, the happy shouting of bridegrooms from their weddings and of young men from their feasts of song. Blessed are you, L-rd, who makes the bridegroom and the bride rejoice together.

Baruch Ata HaShem Elokainu Melech HaOlam, Boreh Pri HaGafen.
Blessed are you, L-rd our G-d, the sovereign of the world, creator of the fruit of the vine.

The seven blessings are recited by the rabbi over a full cup of wine. Notice, they begin with praising G-d for His creation, the creation of the human being, and continue with praise for the creation of the human as a "two part creature": *man and woman.* These blessings express the hope of the new couple to rejoice together forever as though they are Adam and Eve in the Garden of Eden before the fall. The rabbi ends with *"Baruch Ata HaShem Elokainu Melech HaOlam, Boreh Pri HaGafen,"* meaning, "Blessed are you, L-rd our G-d, the sovereign of the world, creator of the fruit of the vine." He includes a prayer for Jerusalem to be fully rebuilt and restored with the Temple in its midst and the Jewish people within her gates. The couple drinks the wine.

The Breaking of the Wine Glass

The groom then breaks the glass by crushing it under his foot. The origin of this custom dates back to ancient times. The cup that the bride and groom share is a covenantal cup; it is broken to declare, "No one will ever drink from this cup but my bride!" Some say, tongue in cheek, this may be the last time the groom gets to "put his foot down". The band plays, and the guests break out into dancing with cries of *"Mozel Tov*[1]*!"*

---

[1] Hebrew for "Good luck" or "Congratulations!"

Cheder Yichud

The couple is now formally or publically married and is accompanied by dancing guests to the *cheder yichud*, "the room of privacy". For the first time, they are alone in a closed room together, an intimacy reserved only for a married couple. And, according to many Jewish authorities, being alone together is a requirement of the legal act of marriage. The couple's entry into the room must be observed by the two witnesses of the marriage. While the bride and groom are alone, the guests will sit down to eat a festive meal. The meal is preceded by a ritual washing of hands and a blessing over the bread.

When the newly conceived couple returns to join their guests, the band plays, the couple joins the festivities, and they are announced as Mr. and Mrs. Everyone joins in dancing around them. Enhancing the joy of the newlyweds, large circles are formed around the "King and Queen." The two have become one!

The meal ends with the *Birchas Hamazon*, Grace after Meals; and again, the seven blessings are recited over wine that is shared by the new couple. The couple is then released, filled with hope and most of all the anticipation of future children—the continuation of the Hebrew generations, and the Covenant blessings of Abraham's seed.

It seems our journey has begun with great pomp and ceremony as well. Our Hebrew wedding, or our Ketubah with Hashem, probably has you asking many questions. *What does this wedding have to do with me?* Let it digest as we continue.

Chapter Five: Thinking like a Hebrew

When one realizes the Bible is written from a Middle Eastern point of view, all of Scripture, even the Brit Hadesha (The New Testament), becomes clearer.

In order to think like a Hebrew, one needs to grasp how the Jewish family still lives today. At the center of their life is the Sh'ma. The Sh'ma is based on the first commandment and is found in Deuteronomy 6:4-9.

> *Hear, O Israel: The L-rd our G-d, the L-rd is one. Love the L-rd your G-d with all your heart and with all your soul and with all your strength. These commandments that I give you today are to be on your hearts. Impress them on your children. Talk about them when you sit at home and when you walk along the road, when you lie down and when you get up. Tie them as symbols on your hands and bind them on your foreheads. Write them on the doorframes of your houses and on your gates. (NIV)*

Hung on every doorpost in Israel is a Mezuzah. A Mezuzah is a small, decorated container which holds the Sh'ma and a scroll of the Ten Commandments. The Sh'ma Blessing is the central prayer in the Jewish prayer book called the Siddur, and it is often the first prayer a Jewish child learns:

Sh'ma Yis'ra'eil Adonai Eloheinu Adonai echad.
Hear, O Israel, the L-rd is our G-d, the L-rd is One.

Barukh sheim k'vod malkhuto l'olam va'ed.
Blessed be the Name of His glorious kingdom for ever and ever.

V'ahav'ta eit Adonai Elohekha b'khol l'vav'kha uv'khol naf'sh'kha uv'khol m'odekha.
And you shall love the L-rd your G-d with all your heart and with all your soul and with all your might.

V'hayu had'varim ha'eileh asher anokhi m'tzav'kha hayom al l'vavekha
And these words that I command you today shall be in your heart.

V'shinan'tam l'vanekha v'dibar'ta bam
And you shall teach them diligently to your children

B'shiv't'kha b'veitekha uv'lekh't'kha vaderekh uv'shakh'b'kha uv'kumekha
When you sit at home, and when you walk along the way, and when you lie down and when you rise up

Uk'shar'tam l'ot al yadekha v'hayu l'totafot bein einekha.
And you shall bind them as a sign on your hand, and they shall be for frontlets between your eyes

Ukh'tav'tam al m'zuzot beitekha uvish'arekha.
And you shall write them on the doorposts of your house and on your gates.

To fully understand the significance of what is the main purpose of this book, you must first understand how it applies to you. Let's start by taking a few steps away from our Greek thinking and toward the thinking of our spiritual fathers. Exodus chapter twenty begins the account of what Gentiles refer to as "the law". Given by G-d, and through His finger written on two stone tablets, Jews understand that the law is good.

> *Wherefore the law is holy, and the commandment holy, and just, and good. — Romans 7:12*

Israel lovingly refers to these commandments as G-d's *Torah* or instruction [Exodus 31:18].

1. I am the L-rd your G-d who brought you out of slavery in Egypt
2. You shall have no other gods but me
3. You shall not misuse the name of the L-rd your G-d
4. You shall remember and keep the Sabbath day holy
5. Honor your father and mother
6. You shall not murder
7. You shall not commit adultery
8. You shall not steal
9. You shall not bear false witness against thy neighbor
10. You shall not covet

What we Westerners call "The Ten Commandments" begins Israel's time of teaching in which G-d gave them 613 commandments. Because modern Christianity teaches that Jesus came to do away with these laws, most Believers never give them a second thought. In truth, the majority of G-d's holy laws are simply "be good to one another, take care of each other, be moral, and be set apart". The rest detail the ways in which the Father wants to be worshipped. This is why Y'shua Himself stated that the law could be summed up in two commandments.

> *Jesus said unto him, Thou shalt love the L-rd thy G-d with all thy heart, and with all thy soul, and with all thy mind. This is the first and great commandment. And the second is like unto it, Thou shalt love thy neighbour as thyself. On these two commandments hang all the law and the prophets. — Matthew 22:37-40*

Christianity in the West calls these "heavy," "burdensome," and something to be "freed from". Westerners are a people who crave freedom. Still, the Code of Laws of the United States of America is 200,000 pages long (according to online sources); and in 2010, 40,627 *new* laws were added to the books. While everyone but the U.S. government would argue that this is far too many, most Americans consider themselves to be a free people. Wanting a *truly* free people, our smart, incredible G-d designed an entire system of life and government in only six hundred and thirteen laws!

The law of G-d has not been forsaken by all. There are those around the world who gratefully join with Israel and her covenants and walk in the ways of G-d's Chosen. The people of Israel keep G-d's law—not to be His, but because they are His.

In Israel today, the devout Jewish person attempts to keep the laws of G-d at the center of his life, teaching the commandments diligently to his children. A Jew keeps the law because he is a Jew, and he believes this is his heritage and his service to G-d. Israel's salvation at Rosh Hashanah and Yom Kippur is for the entire nation, not just the individual. The Jew keeps the Law—not to be family, but because he is family.

Dangers of "Greek Thinking"

As Emperor of Rome in 320 AD, Constantine had tremendous influence. He converted to Christianity in the interest of his own political endeavors which he then demanded that the empire adopt. In short, he *Hellenized*[1] Christianity in his pursuit of politics, and he sought to annihilate all Hebrew customs and traditions. But he wasn't the first. The way was paved for Constantine, and according to Bacchiocchi[2], "under Vespasian (A.D. 69-79) both the Sanhedrin and the high priesthood were abolished; and under Hadrian . . . the practice of the Jewish religion and particularly Sabbath keeping were outlawed."

---

[1] The governing law of that day was pagan which was forced upon Israel. The penalty was slavery or death if one did not relinquish all things Judaism.
[2] Samuel Bacchiocchi, "The Rise of Sunday Observance in Early Christianity," in **The Sabbath in Scripture and History**, ed. Kenneth A. Strand (Washington, D.C.: Review and Herald, 1982)

After Constantine, the assault continued. Those who observed the Sabbath were persecuted by the Catholic Church. When the Jesuit St. Francis Xavier arrived in India, he immediately began an inquisition complaining to the Pope of "Jewish wickedness".

> *"The Jewish wickedness of which Xavier complained was evidently the Sabbath-keeping among those native Christians as we shall see in our next quotation. When one of these Sabbath-keeping Christians was taken by the Inquisition he was accused of having *Judaized*; which means having conformed to the ceremonies of the Mosaic Law; such as not eating pork, hare, fish without scales, of having attended the solemnization of the Sabbath."* [Account of the Inquisition at Goa, Dellon, p.56. London, 1815]

> *"Of an hundred persons condemned to be burnt as Jews, there are scarcely four who profess that faith at their death; the rest exclaiming and protesting to their last gasp that they are Christians, and have been so during their whole lives."* [p.64]

According to Good News Magazine, May/June 2006, Constantine's main objective was to universalize the church—blending all elements of popular religion into one cohesive mode of worship. While he was not successful in permanently wiping out Judaism, he did annihilate the purity of the early church and replace their Jewish Messiah with a blond-haired blue-eyed Jesus.

Constantine was a devout worshipper of the sun god, and this worship is reflected in many of our traditions today. Years after his supposed conversion to Christianity, Constantine minted gold coins with himself on one side and the "unconquered Sol [sun]" on the other.

Constantine's sun worship is the reason Christians now worship on Sunday—the first day of the week and a day dedicated to honoring the sun. Constantine's willful hatred of "all things Jewish" made it very difficult on those Jews and Christians who continued to keep the biblical Sabbath on the seventh day of the week (a century later the Council of Laodicea would outlaw Sabbath-keeping and Christian observance of the biblical Holy Days). According to British historian, Paul Johnson, *"Many Christians did not make a clear distinction between this sun-cult [Mithraism] and their own [religion]."* Although a polluting of the early church happened even earlier than Constantine, after he had his way, Christians held their services on Sunday and had their nativity-feast on the twenty-fifth of December—the birthday of the sun at the winter solstice.

At the Council of Nicea (A.D. 325), authorities replaced biblical Passover with Easter—named for the wife of the sun god. Easter existed already as a popular holiday rooted in detestable fertility rituals and human sacrifice. Applauding their decision to shun Passover and embrace the furthering of sun god worship, Constantine announced: *"It appeared an unworthy thing that in the celebration of this most holy feast [Easter] we should follow the practice of the Jews, who have impiously defiled their hands with enormous sin, and are, therefore, deservedly afflicted with blindness of soul . . . Let us then have nothing in common with the detestable Jewish crowd"* [Eusebius, *Life of Constantine 3,* 18-19, *Nicene and Post-Nicene Fathers,* 1979, second series, Vol. 1, pp. 524-525].

"How could the Christian Church, apparently quite willingly, accommodate this weird megalomaniac [Constantine]? Was there a conscious bargain? Which side benefited most from this unseemly marriage between Church and State? ... Did the empire surrender to Christianity, or did Christianity prostitute itself to the empire?" [A History of Christianity; Johnson; 1976, pp. 67-69].

Considering the differences between Christianity of today and the "Christianity" of Jesus Christ and the apostles, we can clearly see that something treacherous has happened. One can trace much of that treachery to Constantine and his abhorrence of the ways of G-d. For me, this is amazingly eye opening. *That's what happened,* not only to The Feasts and Convocations in the Temple, but to the early church as well!

Still, a remnant has remained. Daniel Augsburger concluded his chapter, *The Sabbath and L-rd's Day During the Middle Ages,* with:

> *"But also, all throughout that period there were groups of people who, either through the example of the Jews or because of their study of the Scriptures, attempted to keep the day that Jesus and the apostles had kept. For obvious reasons we know little about their number or their names, but their presence shows that in every age there were some who attempted to place the Word of G-d above the traditions of men."*

Westerners have a Hellenized or Greek version of the Judeo Christian faith—a *bad copy*. This modernized version of Christianity does not simply add new twists, it is dramatically changed from the original. If you have a Western mindset, you have probably bypassed some of the greatest blessings of all time. *Oh! Oh! This writer is out to get me!* No, but in an earnest attempt to get us back to our Hebraic roots, let's continue. Get ready for some radical paradigm shifts!

What is a Western Mind Set?

The term *Western mindset* applies to anyone living west of the Middle East who has developed and believed a version of the first church *after* it was Hellenized. Concerned about where I'm going with this, you may insist, "So what if I have a Western mind set? I'm still a believer!" Yes, of course you are! If you follow Jesus, you are a Believer. We have a supernatural G-d; and, thanks to the Holy Spirit who edited the whole thing in our favor, we have received the message the disciples proclaimed. But after the third century, much of the original first church was lost and much of Judaism was erased. Thinking with a Western mindset deletes the core of Hebrew life and thought completely. This lost mindset thinks in terms of community, relationship, and right living before the Almighty.

Westerners use and believe the Greek philosophical, intellectual approach. The Greeks translated and then re-engineered the original texts, imposing on the original writings a Hellenized version which circulated throughout the Roman Empire. The Hebrew person remains practical in his approach to Hashem; he is interested in living a way of life according to the Torah, obeying the One True G-d, and giving G-d glory through all aspects of his life. The Hebrew person is more interested in how one is to treat their neighbor than he is with diagnosing life, love, and G-d according to scientific rules and regulations—the Greek way.

Westerners are predominantly concerned with denominations, creeds, doctrinal statements, and systematic theologies. This mode of thinking is thoroughly, utterly *Greek*. It is not the way of the Hebrew. Abraham Herschel, a rabbi and one of the leading Jewish theologians and philosophers of the 20th century, explained this kind of Western thinking about G-d.

"The categories within which philosophical reflection about religion has been operating, are derived from Athens rather than from Jerusalem".

In our time, the Holy Spirit—the Ruach Ha Kodesh—is doing much to restore the Body to its first foundations. If we are to understand the Bible and what it means to be a follower of *Y'shua, ha Mashiach* (Jesus, the Messiah), then we need to understand it Hebraically—not Hellenistically. This will require a philosophical and intellectual paradigm shift on our part. It will mean coming at Scripture from a different angle than we have most likely been accustomed. It will mean learning to think like an Israelite and accepting the fact that the Bible we know today was written to people with an entirely different worldview.

What is the difference?

To truly grasp the Hebrew culture of Biblical times is to experience a type of culture shock—to travel back to a time we haven't known. Remember, the Bible was written during the pre-scientific age. Their view of the world was unlike ours. Their values and perceptions were also radically different. We live in a high tech world, they plowed with oxen and hands. We are immersed in and enlightened by TV, satellites, computers, and books. They did not read, did not have the Bible to follow, and had a bit of a superstitious bent.

We have GPS; they used the stars. We have the Tenach[3] and the Brit Hadesha; they taught their children as their parents had taught them—through words passed down from generation to generation. We have preachers, even movies, to give life to their story; they lived it.

As we go along, we will attempt to embrace the point of view from which the Bible was written in the first place. We will seek to reestablish a new kind of relationship with G-d by thinking with a Hebraic mind. What may have seemed merely ritualistic (or even legalistic) to us in the past, will, when examined through new eyes, gain immense and exciting meaning.

---

[3] Tanakh is Hebrew for many books in the Old Testament which were relayed by oral tradition. The Five Books of Moses, the Prophets, and the Writings make up the Tanakh, or our version: Tenach

To Think Like Y'shua is to Think "Jewish"

Y'shua was circumcised and named on the 8th day.

And when eight days were completed for him to be circumcised, his name was called Y'shua. —Luke 2:21

He was dedicated to G-d in the Temple.

And when the days of her cleansing according to the law of Moses were completed, they brought him to Jerusalem to present him to The Almighty, as it has been written in the law of The Almighty, "Every male who opens the womb shall be called set-apart to The Almighty and to give an offering according to what is said in the law of The Almighty. And when they had accomplished all according to the law of The Almighty, they returned to Galilee, to their city Nazareth." —Luke 2: 22-24

Y'shua was raised in a Jewish home. He memorized the Sh'ma, the Torah, and He could sing the songs of Shabbat. He did these things because, in the days Y'shua walked the earth, all Hebrew boys memorized the Sh'ma and the first five books of Scripture.

As a youth, He was learned and showed such great knowledge (gained from study and reading because He walked fully the human existence) that he astounded the rabbis and scribes. During His walk on this earth, Y'shua also kept all of the Feasts of Israel.

> *And his parents went to Jerusalem every year at the <u>Festival of the Passover</u>. And when he was twelve years old, they went up to Jerusalem according to the practice of the festival... And it came to be that they found Him in the Temple, sitting in the midst of the teachers, both listening to them and asking them questions. —Luke 2:41-46*
>
> *And on the <u>Feast of Unleavened Bread</u> the taught ones came to Y'shua, saying to him, "Where do you wish us to prepare for you to eat the Passover?"*
> *—Matthew 26:17*
>
> *And the festival of the Jews was near, <u>the Festival of Booths-Tabernacles</u>... and about the middle of the festival Y'shua went up into the Temple, and he was teaching. —John 7:2*
>
> *Then came the <u>Feast of Dedication</u> at Jerusalem. It was winter and Jesus was in the Temple area walking Solomon's Colonnade. – John 10:22-23*

Y'shua not only observed the Feasts in the way we generally think; although He was conceived supernaturally, Y'shua experienced every natural stage of pregnancy. As a preborn, He felt every growth event in the womb just as everyone who has ever been born. Therefore, He experienced each Feast before He was born, just as we did!

Chapter Six: Shabbat

My first experience in Israel was anti-climactic. A parade would have been nice! I arrived at Ben Gurion Tel Aviv airport after a very exhausting twenty-two hour trip and the nine hour time difference. I went straight to the passport station only to be told to *go over there*—to stand in an entirely empty terminal, all by myself, for another hour.

Someone finally came from the Absorption Department to take me through the formal immigration process and give me the legal papers and instructions which all Oleh HaKodesh (new immigrants) are given. After listening to someone explain that mitt full of Hebrew paperwork in English and tell me what all those signatures were for, I was an official citizen of Israel! After many *"Mozel Tov"*s, I was ushered to a waiting cab that would take me to my new home.

My apartment was in the city of Modi'in, a community halfway between Jerusalem and Tel Aviv. I had finally arrived in the Promised Land, but with no one to meet me—no band playing rousing Jewish songs, no flag waving. After all of my longing and effort, I was home. Home, but alone. Alone, but excited. After all, I am the child of the King, I have royal blood running in my veins, and I had just arrived in the King's Land! But even royalty need sleep. So, I went to bed only to awaken late on Friday afternoon.

Shabbat

Shabbat is so very important to life in Israel and to keeping His commandments. Jewish people celebrate the blessings of G-d and family life every Friday evening in a ritual called the Sabbath— or Shabbat. The wife lights the Shabbat candles. The father blesses the wine and bread (similar to communion) in joyfully sung prayers. The children eagerly gather around Papa as he lays hands on every child and blesses them. This is a time to celebrate their relationship with G-d, family, and community, thanking the L-rd for all He has provided.

The Scriptures make it clear that Shabbat happens on Friday at sundown. Why do Westerner's not do this? I am here to tell you that we all have been cheated out of some of the most beautiful experiences and blessings by not following the Hebrew example.

In addition to other Sabbath commands and instructions, there is a command given in Leviticus 23:3 which says:

> *Six days shall work be done: but the seventh day is the Sabbath of rest, an holy convocation; ye shall do no work therein: it is the Sabbath of the L-rd in all your dwellings.*

Shabbat is a time to rest from all work, and most Israelis still honor it. Devout Jews use the time to worship and pray many times a day, but secular Jews head for the beaches to relax. Sunday is the first business day of the Israeli week and everyone is refreshed and eager to begin again. Shabbat bookmarks the end of the work week and makes time for worship and family fellowship.

In contrast, Westerners work feverishly for five or six days and worship on Sundays—if they make it to church. Today, most Westerners are so exhausted they use Sunday to relax in front of the TV or work around the house. Monday always comes too soon. But the Torah is clear: G-d created, and then He rested! He then decreed that His people do the same.

So there I was, in the Holy Land, just waking in time for the beginning of the day of rest—evening to evening. Everything was closed, no exceptions, and no food! I knocked on the door across the way from mine to introduce myself and to hopefully eat.

They had just started their Shabbat, the candles already lit, but they warmly invited me to join them and made room for me in their humble home. Mr. Comade wore his yarmulke; and with his prayer books in hand, he called his wife to begin. Just as she settled in her chair, he read fervently and then raised the wine glass and blessed it. Next, he filled tiny glasses and passed them to each of us. He continued to pray and the others responded in Hebrew.

"Amein."

Everyone jumped up to wash their hands, praying a blessing on the hands that made the meal and asking that our own hands would be as servants to the L-rd. Hands are washed by splashing water from a container used only for washing hands on Shabbat. The water is poured over the hands three times and prayer is continuous during the washing. After washing, we then returned to the table without saying a word. No one is to speak until after the blessing of the bread. The bread was raised up high and blessed, then passed to each of us.

The table was spread with small dishes of garnishes: olives, and special foods such as eggplant, humus, and coleslaw. Then salad was served after the homemade chicken soup was finished. A platter of chicken followed, little boiled potatoes and rice mixed with green vegetables, too. Dessert was a pudding, like tapioca—served with coffee. The entire evening embodied the Shabbat. The mood was festive, full of debating and laughter. The children sang prayers, and the father laid hands on them to bless each one. After we had finished eating, prayer books were again handed out and we prayed and read silently for a while. They told me to call on them for any help I might need, and after chatting into the evening, it was time to go—in peace and with a heart so full it might have burst. I was home, finally. I was family.

The entire Israeli workweek is different from other parts of the world. Shabbat actually starts when you see the first three stars after sundown and lasts all day Saturday until evening at sundown. No one works or does business.

You can hear a pin drop. All cars, buses, and trains just stop; nothing is open, and all is quiet. The family gathers to light the Shabbat (Sabbath) candles and enjoy a wonderful meal together. Everyone participates. The food has been prepared well in advance so that according to Scriptures, "no servile work" is done on Shabbat. One is to enjoy only rest and worship. In fact, Shabbat is so important to the life of a Jewish family, to the life of those seeking to follow in the footsteps of our fathers, we must grasp its meaning before even attempting to investigate the Feasts.

Chapter Seven: The Feasts of the L-rd

The L-rd G-d of Israel commanded the Israelites to celebrate many miracles and historical events, most importantly seven Holy Feasts called Convocations. These Convocations are the L-rd's punctuation marks—memory-makers in the lives of the Israelites. We can see now that they are also prophetic rehearsals of Y'shua's first and second coming! Right off the bat, He commanded His people to keep the Sabbath, live by the Sh'ma, and celebrate all of The Feasts of the L-rd.

> *And the L-rd spake unto Moses saying, Speak unto the children of Israel, and say unto them, concerning The Feasts of the L-RD, which ye shall proclaim to be holy convocations, even these are my feasts. Six days shall work be done, but the seventh day is the Sabbath of rest, an holy convocation; ye shall do no work therein: it is the Sabbath of the L-rd in all your dwellings.*
> *—Leviticus 23:1*

What does this have to do with us? This is our religion! There is only One True G-d—the G-d of Abraham, Isaac, and Jacob!

The Hebrew people of the Bible were a simple people—mostly, farmers, shepherds, or nomads. They knew the seasons of the year well. They used stars to navigate, they understood the seasons of rain and the seasons of drought. Hashem guided them. He punctuated their seasons with feasts and convocations. These were Hebrew memory-makers—holy memorization tools. These markers of time were to be revisited yearly, teaching the family how to worship. Fathers handed down the events to sons who in turn handed them down to their sons—mishnah[3].

Detailed instructions for each feast can be found in the Torah, expressly in the books of Leviticus and Deuteronomy. This collection of ancient Hebrew writings form the basis of Jewish religious law—also consisting of the early scriptural interpretations and the later commentaries (Mishnah) on them.

The Holy Feasts of the L-rd are:

1. Passover (Pesach)
2. Unleavened Bread
3. First Fruits
4. Shavuot (Pentecost)
5. Rosh Hashanah (Feast of Trumpets or Yom Teruah)
6. Yom Kippur
7. Feast of Tabernacles (Sukkot)
8. Chanukah (Feast of Dedication or Festival of Lights)

In Leviticus, we see that there are only seven Feasts of the L-rd—seven convocations were originally given. By adding the later Feast of Chanukah as the eighth convocation, however, an interesting pattern takes shape. And it forms a wonderful possibility! But I'm getting ahead of myself.

---

[3] From repetition or instruction, oral. The first section of the Talmud, being a collection of early oral interpretations of the scriptures as compiled about A.D. 200.

The Hebrew word for appointment is *Moed,* which actually means *an appointed time*! Each of The Feasts are *Moeds,* appointments, with G-d! Personally, I don't want to miss a single one.

Feasts in Modern Day

I have tried to find New Testament Scriptures that would nullify The Feasts of the Torah—but to no avail. There is not one scripture which does away with The Feasts, and Y'shua Himself celebrated *all* of The Feasts of the Torah—even including the Feast of Chanukah.

Some mistakenly say that Apostle Paul called them obsolete by referring to the new covenant under Jesus. It is important to remember, though, that Y'shua came <u>not</u> to abolish the law, but to live it fully and beautifully and to be an example for us.

> *"Think not that I am come to destroy the law, or the prophets: I am not come to destroy, but to fulfil. For verily I say unto you, Till heaven and earth pass, one jot or one tittle shall in no wise pass from the law, till all be fulfilled. Whosoever therefore shall break one of these least commandments, and shall teach men so, he shall be called the least in the kingdom of heaven: but whosoever shall do and teach them, the same shall be called great in the kingdom of heaven."*
> —*Matthew 5:17-19*

G-d gave us His Feasts for a reason! Why would *we* not celebrate them? What possible reason could we have for avoiding these meetings and dodging the blessings of G-d?

Chapter Eight: Two Topics

As the inspiration for writing this book, I became aware of two precise topics which seemed to be intertwined.

1. Torah Feasts
2. Development of a Preborn Child

When I first began to see this, I knew something of great importance was here. Frustration took me to my knees. "Please Abba, help me to understand what this is. I want to get it right! What do you want to say?" I heard that sweet and quiet voice answer. *"Write it to my children!"*

Clarifying, He said, "I want you to tell this story to Jews, Gentiles, midwives, Believers, and unbelievers, but especially to your own children. Just write!" So, I began to write; and as I did, the delicious *"Yum!"* moments came. Through tiny bites of revelation, I began to notice things I hadn't seen before.

The ancient Hebrews followed (and still do, today) a lunar[2] calendar. This piqued my interest; because, as a Midwife, I use a lunar cycle to determine the due date of a baby.

---

[2] The lunar calendar is based on the approximately 29.53 day cycle of the moon. The Egyptian calendar has 31 days and follows the sun and the sun G-d

In my initial research, I learned that the tides, growing seasons, menstrual, and birth cycles all seem to be dictated by the power of the lunar system—as are The Torah Feasts. I quickly decided to take a deeper look at the Torah.

I got out my midwifery books, the Torah, and a concordance. I cranked up the computer and began to follow a line of study. As one thing led to another, there seemed to be a timeline developing. I mentioned earlier that I had two topics: Feasts of the Torah and the Development of a Preborn Child. I knew these were my topics, topics that would meld to become one cohesive answer. Overwhelmed, I returned to my knees. "Please Hashem", help me to understand." It was at this point that I first heard Him add the word *"journey"*. By adding the word "journey," my assignment had changed into something I could see.

1. **Journey of the Chosen People**
2. **Journey of the Preborn**

I counted the days between these eight celebrations (between Passover and Chanukah). I found, though it practically knocked me over to do so, that there are exactly two-hundred and eighty days from the first through the last festival. To begin backing my opening statement: it takes that same number of days, two-hundred and eighty, from the release of a human egg to the fullness of time—birth! I also found that each Holy Feast fell on exactly the same days which are important in the development of a preborn—through each stage of gestation, until birth. Wow! Well, there's a good start. As a midwife, a light bulb went off in my head. That was my first big "*Yum!*"

I could barely contain my excitement; still, I needed to dig deeper. I wanted to prove what I already felt from the L-rd to be true. While we were in our mothers' wombs, we—all of humanity—met each Moed *or* appointment, and experienced each one of the Torah Feasts before we were born! In the ancient Hebrew language, there is no such word as coincidence. This fact gave me the initial courage I needed to continue my digging, and *oh* the excitement at what I would find!

I turned my attention to Passover. The Israelites were *released* from bondage in Egypt. During a woman's menstrual cycle, an egg is *released*. "Release" is the key word: Passover is the first Feast *and* the start of gestation!

The true point of this writing is the eight Feasts and prenatal development as they mirror each other. As I'd merely begun my research, these events already seemed to match each other in such a unique way. I asked the L-rd to help me put it all on paper when I discovered a third topic—the Journey of the Bride. "Yikes! What do you mean L-rd, how does it fit in? I don't know the first thing about how to do this." Lamenting, "Please have someone else do it, not me. The first two topics are difficult enough. To add yet a third topic is going to take a miracle." He just whispered again, "Write!" And while I pondered, I also wondered "What about all my Jewish friends, especially here in Israel? Will the powers that be come get me? Will the devout or anti-missionary law deport me?"

Behold, to obey is better than sacrifice. — Samuel 15:22

G-d is no respecter of persons—color, gender, or creed. Our Creator, our Abba, is sovereign! If we line up the journey of the Chosen People with the journey of the preborn, a marvelous story begins to appear. And a third journey, not to be overlooked, is that of Believers or the Believing Church—the Journey of the Bride. I wondered if she also follows this same pattern and was on a long journey which could be seen in The Feasts!

Chapter Nine: "Everything Old is New Again?"

At the Jewish wedding I recently attended, I was seated next to a very lovely couple from the UK. We all had our plates full of wonderful kosher delicacies. As dinner conversation, the topic turned to our occupations. My being a midwife, and their having trouble conceiving, they were very interested in my line of work. I gave them some referrals in England, jotted down titles of good books; and then, I thought I'd found an excellent opportunity to try out my *bright new idea*. I began to share the parallel charts of the Chosen's journey and the journey of the preborn. My excitement was met with polite but empty smiles.

Do you know how disappointing it is to try to share your *bright new idea* only to be passed off or dismissed? Oh yes, they politely pretended to listen, but they wore glassy eyed, off in the distance looks while synchronously nodding their heads. Eventually, I lost them to the dance floor.

The tune being played was **"Everything Old is New Again"**. My thoughts drifted over the nice background sounds of song and laughter. *What had gone wrong?* I wondered. My intention was only to share *this bright new idea*. I thought they would easily "get it." Boy, was I wrong!

Have you ever heard the song *"Everything Old is New Again"*? That little ditty kept going around and around in my head for days after the wedding. It's a catchy tune which talks about everything old fashioned that is still oddly familiar. The old things do re-cycle and come around to become new and stylish again—just like this information. It is very old but has also become miraculously new!

Would you agree that we live in the age of information? We have robots doing work in factories. We watch international TV, use high tech computers, phone people on Skype, and *Google* the answers to our questions. We've been to space, discovered DNA, armed and disarmed nuclear weapons. We know things now that even ten years ago we wouldn't have believed possible. You'd think that with all this information and increased education we would be the smartest people on the earth. Well, it may be new information, but we are still acting in a very old way.

Why are we still allowing genocide? Why do we still choose to abort our precious babies? The freedom of prayer is no longer allowed in our schools or public places, and we wonder why we are on the brink of nuclear war. What is wrong with us? What is wrong with our thinking? Are human beings just incapable of sustaining peace, joy, fairness, and the very love they scream for?

The Bible records the same problems all the way back to the beginning of time. The Old Testament is filled with prophets lamenting the people of G-d to come back into right relationship with Hashem. He chose a people who said they would follow Him no matter what; but almost in the next breath, that same people turned to a lifeless golden idol. Even after Hashem had done many miracles for them, they ran backward to something they thought safer and more familiar. They trusted Egypt more than the G-d of their fathers. Not much has changed today. Still, our benevolent, loving Creator forgave them and continues to forgive, teach, and lead His people back to Himself.

He called them His Chosen and began grooming them to be His wife. These wonderful accounts found in the Torah are not just stories of *dos* and *don'ts* but a diary of G-d's love and patient guidance of a people He chose for all eternity. It's His story; and it's your story, too.

Chapter Ten: The Midwives and Moses

The Israelites were living under excruciating bondage in Egypt. According to records, they were in Egypt for 430 years. An old tradition tells the story of Pharaoh having a dream in which there was a set of hanging scales. In his dream, he saw the scales off balance with all of Egypt on one side and a lamb on the other—outweighing Egypt. The magicians who interpreted the dream thought it meant that a male child would soon be born to Israel who would destroy the whole of Egypt. With that in mind, the fearful Pharaoh decreed the killing of every baby boy [Dakes Annotated Reference Bible; June 1989].

The great Pharaoh of Egypt spoke directly to the Hebrew midwives, Shiphrah (in Hebrew meaning Beautiful) and Puah (in Hebrew meaning Splendid). These two Hebrew midwives were personally called to the throne room where Pharaoh spoke to them face to face and said,

> *"When ye do the office of a midwife to the Hebrew women and see them upon the stools, if it be a son then ye shall kill him: but if it be a daughter, then she shall live." –Exodus 1:15-16*

A midwife's specialty is delivering babies and tending to families. Midwives love babies and their families. Shiphrah and Puah had birthed many of the Hebrews living at the time, and their sincere objective was always the well-being and safety of mother and baby. Now, suddenly, they were called to a meeting and given an ultimatum by the king: *Do this thing, or die!* This mindboggling order cut cross-grain to their life's work—to their very being.

These two ordained midwives were G-d fearing. In a time when most of Israel had forgotten the name of their G-d, Shiphrah and Puah understood the character of G-d; they knew the fifth commandment even though they did not yet know it *as* the fifth commandment: "You shall not murder". They feared Almighty G-d more than they feared any man, so they began to devise a plan. *"What if we don't deliver the babies? What if we are busy somewhere else, too far away to get to the births? After all, Hebrew women are accustomed to doing hard labor and their bodies are in great condition. They're used to squatting, pushing, carrying heavy materials, and hauling loads uphill. They simply give birth before we get there!"* These righteous women obeyed their G-d rather than the Pharaoh, and Scripture goes on to tell us:

> *"But the midwives feared G-d, and did not as the king of Egypt commanded them, but saved the men children alive" –Exodus 1:17-18.*

Months passed, and again Shiphrah and Puah were asked to appear before the Pharaoh. No doubt he was more than a little perturbed to learn they had not killed *any* baby boys. Right then and there, he could have had their heads cut off for not obeying his orders, but Shiphrah and Puah responded, *"but they were born before we got there, sir."*

G-d covered them with great favor; the Pharaoh believed their story and spared their lives! But more than that, Scripture tells us that G-d greatly rewarded the midwives' obedience.

> *Therefore G-d dealt well with the midwives, and the people multiplied and waxed very mighty. And it came to pass that because the midwives feared G-d, that He made them houses. –Exodus 2:20*

It is in this same tumultuous time period that we read of the birth of a very special Hebrew baby. You can read of the birth of Moses in Exodus 2:1-9

By faith, Moses' mother placed her infant son in a crocodile infested river as the only means of prolonging his life. And before any harm could come to him, Moses was found by the Pharaoh's daughter who unknowingly gave him back to his own mother for the remainder of his infancy because she needed someone to nurse him. Not only this, but Moses' mother was paid for the privilege. Extraordinary!

When Moses was four or five, he was returned to the Egyptian princess. Isn't it just like G-d to put a Hebrew boy in the middle of the enemy camp to learn everything he could of the Egyptians? He enjoyed the best education in science, engineering, law, and medicine. After all, he was being raised as a prince. But Moses was also a daily witness to the harsh treatment of G-d's Chosen. At the right time, G-d awakened Moses' Hebrew heart and used him to orchestrate the Sh'mitah —*release* of the Hebrew people. We begin the next part of our journey, with *the release*— the Passover.

The Feast of Passover is actually three feasts in one. First, is the feast we call "Passover". The following day is the Feast of Unleavened Bread. Then, in the middle of this Feast is the Feast of First Fruits. In the twenty-third chapter of Leviticus, we find The Feasts, convocations, and sacrifices which the L-rd G-d commanded the Children of Israel to obey and observe. They are appointments with G-d—*Moeds*. As the Hebrew people journeyed out of Egypt, they experienced many milestones. These significant events in the history of the Hebrews act as bookmarks, or punctuation marks, in time. The first punctuation mark is Passover.

Although G-d has taught His children His ways from the beginning, a long enslaved, Egypt-tainted Israel had all but forgotten their G-d. The Law given by G-d through Moses was a written handbook direct from the manufacturer. Specific directions for each Feast can be found in Leviticus and Deuteronomy. The Law was passed to Moses during the Hebrews' sanctifying wilderness experience, almost immediately after their release from Egypt. It reveals the promises of Hashem's covenant with His people.

In the Torah, Passover and the immediately following feasts are explained. The Children of G-d are instructed that on the fifteenth day, the day following the Passover (*Pesach*) sacrifice, they should not have any leavened bread in their homes. This cleansing was to last for seven-days as a festival unto the L-rd. He gave a command to search for and remove leaven from the house in preparation for the Festival of Unleavened Bread. In Hebrew, this ceremony is called *Bedikat HaMetz* which means "the search for leaven." In the Scriptures, leaven is often, though not always, an allegory for sin.

Chapter Eleven: The Big Picture

When I first began to see what I've outlined in the next chapters, I was overwhelmed. I made copious amounts of notes; and eventually, I simplified them and ended up with the following charts. On the next pages, you will find comparison charts that illustrate each point. When I compared my knowledge of each feast with my knowledge of each stage of pregnancy, what emerged simply blew my mind! G-d is a G-d of grand design!

Beginning at Passover to complete a perfect pregnancy year, both the preborn and the Chosen travel a similar path. Their journey moves them from dramatic event to dramatic event and eventually to a dedicated life. And, for both the preborn and the Chosen of G-d, each event is accompanied by incredible changes and developments. I believe G-d has hidden, in plain sight, His masterful blueprint. When I compared these journeys, it was all I could do just to lean back and digest what I was seeing. Each Torah Feast corresponds very closely to an event in prenatal growth; and there is no Hebrew word for *"coincidence"*. As I moved along, I continued to see more and more. Do you? Can you see the parallels developing? The evidence is there, enough to firmly believe: He knew you, and you met with Him, before you were even born!

> *Before I formed you in the womb I knew you; Before you were born I sanctified you; And I ordained you a prophet to the nations.* — *Jeremiah 1:5 NIV*

Event 1:
Month 1, Day 14
Day 1

|

Feast of Passover:
Hebrews released from Egypt

|

Release

|

Preborn Development:

|

Release of Ova

|

Chapter Twelve: Passover

Parallel Events between the Journey of the Hebrews and the Journey of the Preborn: Event 1—The Release

Journey of the People

When Pharaoh denied Moses' request for the release of the Chosen People, the L-rd brought ten plagues upon the land. Egypt was devastated; still, Pharaoh's heart remained hard. When the tenth and final plague was unleashed, it took the lives of every firstborn in Egypt, including the Pharaoh's own son. Throughout the carnage, the Israelites were completely protected. Why? They obeyed G-d who had carefully instructed them. He told them to take the blood of a perfect lamb and place it on the door posts of their homes. For those who obeyed, death passed over them. Because of demonstrated faith, the Hebrews were saved from their past and released to new life. As a result of the devastation, G-d bent Pharaoh's knee and released the Israelites to their new beginnings. They began their journey to the Promised Land by way of the wilderness. To commemorate their salvation, G-d instructed the people to keep the Feast of Passover. This feast, also known as "the feast of freedom," is still celebrated every year on the fourteenth day of the month of Nisan.

Journey of the Preborn

The journey of a preborn child is a miracle, from the time the egg leaves the ovary until the great celebration at the birth of a full-term child. This journey includes many changes for the ova in transit. In the development of a human baby, the mother ovulates—releasing an egg from her ovary. The process of ovulation happens every month on *the fourteenth day* of her cycle. And so, we have our first parallel!

Event 2:

Day 2

|

Feast of Unleaved Bread :

|

No leaven

|

Preborn Development:

|

Two become one
No leaven

Chapter Thirteen: Feast of Unleavened Bread

Parallel Events between the Journey of the Hebrews and the Journey of the Preborn: Event 2—No sin or leaven

Journey of the People

The Feast of Unleavened Bread is the day after Passover. During this feast, no leaven can be eaten or stored within the home for seven days. Leaven is the word often used in Scripture to describe sin. Although they did not know it yet, the ancient Hebrew people were being cleansed of sin, dying to 400 years of idolatry and becoming joined together in covenant with their G-d.

Journey of the Preborn

The ova has been released, but there can now be no leaven in its environment. No bacteria, nor too much acid or not enough—the home of the ova must be perfect and clean. If there is bacteria near the ova, the organism will devour it. The ova must be fertilized in this environment within twenty-four hours. If not fertilized, it will die and simply pass on with menses. However, if the egg is fertilized, the original forms of each—the egg and sperm have died or changed from their original form to become something altogether different. Like the Israelites with their G-d, the two have made a covenant with one another. No longer are they single forms of energy. Individually, they each carried twenty-three chromosomes; but now, they've merged together to carry forty-six chromosomes of the precious DNA of a brand new preborn person.

Event 3:

Day 4

|

Feast of First Fruits:

|

Hebrews waved to freedom--Wave offering offered to G-d

|

Preborn Development:
|
Zygote waved through to uterus by Cilia/Fimbria

Chapter Fourteen: Feast of First Fruits

Parallel Events between the Journey of the Hebrews and the Journey of the Preborn: Event 3 —Wave Offerings

Journey of the People

In Israel, wheat and barley are planted in the fall. All through the winter, there is no sign of growth. Then, in the spring, life breaks forth from the ground. The first-fruits wave offering marks the beginning of the spring barley harvest and the counting period to Shavuot.

> *The L-rd said to Moses, "Speak to the Israelites and say to them: "When you enter the land I am going to give you and you reap its harvest, bring to the priest a sheaf of the first grain you harvest. He is to wave the sheaf before the L-rd so it will be accepted on your behalf; the priest is to wave it on the day after the Sabbath. On the day you wave the sheaf, you must sacrifice as a burnt offering to the L-rd a lamb a year old without defect, together with its grain offering of two-tenths of an ephah of the finest flour mixed with olive oil — a food offering presented to the L-rd, a pleasing aroma — and its drink offering of a quarter of a hin of wine. You must not eat any bread, or roasted or*

new grain, until the very day you bring this offering to your G-d. This is to be a lasting ordinance for the generations to come, wherever you live.
–Leviticus 23:9-14 NIV

When it came time to harvest the spring crop, the first sheaf was to be offered to G-d. The Feast of First Fruits falls within the Feast of Unleavened Bread and is the festival celebration of the barley harvest. During this feast, the first of the harvest is offered to G-d as a Wave Offering. It can also be paralleled that G-d waved the Hebrews through to freedom as they continued their long walk out of Egypt.

Journey of the Preborn

Approximately three days after fertilization, the zygote[1] travels through the fallopian tube. The mechanism which propels it through this part of its journey is a series of hair-like structures (cilia and fimbria) that wave the first fruits of the birthing process along. This waving motion promotes the zygote to arrive in the uterus. Much like the Israelites coming into the land, the zygote (now called an embryo) seeks implantation in the uterus. This all important destination will offer a rich source of nourishment.

---

[1] term for ova and sperm after fertilization

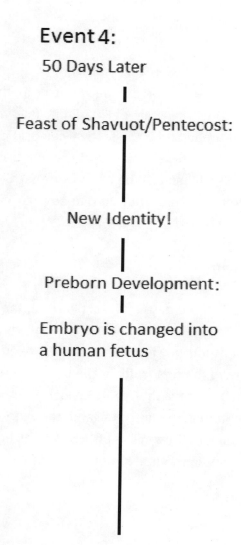

Chapter Fifteen: Shavuot

Parallel Events between the Journey of the Hebrews and the Journey of the Preborn: Event 4 –A New Name

Journey of the People

At the Feast of First Fruits, the farmers brought in the early barley harvest. Then, Israel began to count out fifty days. In the Torah, this is called counting the omer; farmers today still refer to this period of waiting as the growing season. Barley was gathered in the month of Nisan; but before wheat is mature and ready for harvest, fifty more days must pass. Shavuot, also known as Pentecost, actually means fifty ("Pente" from the Greek and "Shavuot" from Hebrew).

> *Ye shall count unto you from the morrow after the Sabbath, from the day that ye brought the sheaf of the wave offering: seven Sabbath shall be complete; Even unto the morrow after the seventh Sabbath shall ye number the fifty days and ye shall offer a new meat offering unto the L-rd.* — Leviticus 23: 15-16

At the marking of fifty days, the L-rd commanded His people to celebrate the latter harvest with a great feast. Remember, the first three commanded feasts were Passover, Unleavened Bread, and First Fruits. Now, at Shavuot, a large harvest of wheat is now ready. This is significant as Shavuot always marks a culmination.

When the law was given through Moses, many of The Feasts lay *ahead* of Israel. These feasts would not be fully realized for the Israelites until they came into the Promised Land. But Shavuot was about a harvest long before the people became farmers in the land G-d would give them. Israel's first Shavuot was about G-d's harvest. On Shavuot, Moses received the Commandments from G-d. The objective of the Passover rescue was realized; and in such, Israel received the full guidelines of their covenant. They also received the deed to the Promised Land as it had been given to their father, Abraham. They received a new identity on this day; on this day, they became a nation and His Bride!

Journey of the Preborn

Fifty days after conception, the embryo makes an incredible change. It is at this time the embryo is transformed into a recognizable human and in medical terms is called a fetus. From the time of conception, many changes have taken place in our preborn. Fifty days ago, our preborn was the first fruit of conception. After conception, it traveled on to implantation in the uterus completing the first three Torah Feasts. But fifty days later, we come to a wonderful moment in the development of the preborn. Science tells us that up until this time the embryo cannot be especially designated or recognized as human. But now, he is recognized as such *and is given a new identity!* At Shavuot, G-d's people were no longer a mass of Hebrews but were in one moment declared the holy nation of Israel; at this same moment, our preborn is no longer a mass of human cells but can now be clearly seen (even to the scientific mind) as one perfect and G-d formed human being.

Event 5:

1st of 7th Month

Feast of Trumpets:

Hear the Trump!

Preborn Development:

Hearing has matured just in time to hear the trump!

Chapter Sixteen: Feast of Trumpets

Parallel Events between the Journey of the Hebrews and the Journey of the Preborn: Event Five—Hear the L-rd!

Journey of the People

Rosh Hashanah means Head of the Year. It is the Civil New Year, and this festival is also called the Feast of Trumpets. The shofar is blown, calling the people to repentance and reminding them that the High Holy days are soon approaching. Yom Teruah, yet another name for this feast, means to turn around or repent. These are indeed the days of repentance. In some synagogues, the call for repentance through the blowing of the shofar is sounded one hundred times! Important to our dissection, one must be able to *hear* in order to respond. Because Yom Teruah is commanded to occur on the first day of the seventh month, and because all new months are heralded by the sighting of a new moon, The Feast of Trumpets is also known as *the hidden Feast*. Until it is upon us, no man knows the day or the hour at which this Feast will occur!

> *On the first day of the seventh month ye shall have a memorial of trumpets, a holy convocation.*
> *— Leviticus 23:15-22*

The long summer growing season is complete, and the late crops are ready for harvest. With this harvest, G-d commanded the children of Israel to make a memorial of trumpets, a holy convocation. Like in the spring, we again have three festivals in one. These fall feasts are known as the High Holy Days and begin with the Feast of Trumpets. Then is Yom Kippur, and lastly is Tabernacles. The ten days in between The Feast of Trumpets and Yom Kippur are called the Days of Awe.

Journey of the Preborn

Within the same span of days as the Feast of Trumpets, the preborn has developed his ability to hear! Preborn children are ready to hear the trump of G-d at the very same time as the Feast of Trumpets! Not only are his ears fully developed at this time, but our preborn has developed the ability to *distinguish,* perhaps even identify between, sounds or voices and remember events from during the pregnancy. Romans ten verse seventeen tells us that faith comes by hearing—the preborn's ears are prepared by G-d just in time for the sounding of the Shofar in the seventh month of gestation! The neurons of the brain have advanced to that of a fully developed newborn; the preborn has become consciously aware while still inside the safety of the womb.

Event 6:
7 1/2 months

Yom Kippur:

　　　Blood sacrifice--life
　　　within the blood!

　　Preborn Development:

　　Hemoglobin-A
　　develops--there is life
　　within the blood!

Chapter Seventeen: Yom Kippur

Parallel Events between the Journey of the Hebrews and the Journey of the Preborn: Event Six—In the Blood

Journey of the People

The ten days between Rosh Hashanah and Yom Kippur are known as both the days of awe and the days of repentance. They are heralded by the blowing of the trumpets. During this time, all the people of Israel reflect and ask for forgiveness from Hashem. On the tenth day of the seventh month is Yom Kippur. It is on this solemn holy day that the High Priest makes atonement or restitution for the entire nation. During the first and second temple periods, the Priest was to offer a blood sacrifice for the remission of sins. The atonement that followed meant true reconciliation between G-d and man. During every High Holiday season, millions of Israelis still pray and fast—the entire nation comes to a halt for twenty-four hours. Their prayers are for forgiveness and the inclusion of their name in the book of life for yet another year. This is a solemn feast that during the temple periods required a blood sacrifice by fire. It is a day of introspection, reflection, and repentance.

"On the tenth day of the seventh month, there shall be a day of atonement, it shall be a holy convocation unto you and ye shall afflict your souls, and offer an offering made by fire unto the L-rd.

> *For whatsoever soul it be that shall not be afflicted in that same day, he shall be cut off from among the people."* — Leviticus 23:23

All of Israel was then to wait as the priest offered a sacrifice to atone for the entire nation's sins. When the lamb was sacrificed, and atonement achieved, the High Priest would say "It is Finished!"

> *For the life of the flesh is in the blood: and I have given it to you upon the altar to make an atonement for your souls: for it is the blood that maketh an atonement for the soul.* – Leviticus 17:11

The Day of Atonement demanded the blood of a perfect lamb. The very word "atonement" *means to be at one with the Creator.* Sin separates us from Him, and blood is required for the remission of sins!

Only the High Priest was commissioned to enter the Holy of Holies to present a blood sacrifice on the altar. This blood sacrifice was not for a single person. It was meant to cleanse the entire nation—all of Israel. People would fast (afflict their souls) and pray for forgiveness while a perfect lamb was sacrificed. This was the only way sins could be forgiven, and the sacrifice was done with great pomp and ceremony. People would remain standing outside of the Tabernacle—some waiting patiently, some anxiously, but all with much trepidation. What if the priest didn't return with good news? What if they weren't forgiven? How could they live with the weight of sin and transgressions so heavy on each one's shoulders? Perhaps many hours passed while they waited and prayed. Then, with great shouts of joy and relief, the priest would appear, standing with hands upraised—praising G-d for another year. Oh, the joy! Oh, the triumph! They were again forgiven, free from all guilt and sin.

Journey of the Preborn

Yom Kippur requires blood. Life is in the blood, and blood is necessary for the remission of sins. In light of this, we come to a strange and even mystical parallel. On or very near the tenth day of the seventh month of gestation—parallel to Yom Kippur—our preborn obtains life within his own blood!

Up to this point, the preborn has hearing and perception capabilities and his eyes have developed to see light within the darkness of the womb. But until now, our preborn has been totally dependent on mother who has supplied him through the umbilical cord. At this particular time in development, remarkable in light of of Yom Kippur, the preborn develops a new component in his own blood called Hemoglobin-A. This component enables the preborn to generate and circulate oxygen, and to do so completely independently of mother. Hemoglobin-A was simply not there or was too immature before this time. But it is ready now! At precisely the tenth day of the seventh month, there is life within his blood!

Event 7:

Just before the 8th month

Feast of Tabernacles:

Hashem dwells with His People

Preborn Development:

Lungs developed-- Hashem tabernacles within!

Chapter Eighteen: Feast of Tabernacles

Parallel Events between the Journey of the Hebrews and the Journey of the Preborn: Event Seven—A Tent for Life

Journey of the People

The Feast of Tabernacles (or Feast of Booths) is also called Sukkot. Eight days long, it is a joyous and everlasting feast!

> *"Then the survivors from all the nations that have attacked Jerusalem will go up year after year to worship the King, the L-rd Almighty, and to celebrate the Festival of Tabernacles."*
> *– Zechariah 14:16 (NIV)*

Beginning on the fifteenth day of the seventh month and lasting for eight days, the Feast of Tabernacles commemorates the Israelites' forty years spent in the wilderness in huts or booths. The nation of Israel celebrates by building replicas of the booths they lived in—understanding that G-d was tenting with them and has never forsaken them. This celebration reminds the people of how they were miraculously cared for in the wilderness [Lev 23:39-40]. Israeli children love this time of thanksgiving with their families inside their cozy, makeshift tents. In Israel, it is still every child's favorite time of year.

Journey of the Preborn

The human body is a temporary place of housing for the Spirit of G-d that animates it and gives it life. It is a tabernacle, if you will. Scripture says we are temples for the Holy Spirit—homes for the breath of G-d; He tabernacles within the tent of our flesh.

> *And the L-rd G-d formed man of the dust of the ground, and breathed into his nostrils and the breath of life; and man became a living soul. – Genesis 2:7*

Eight months in utero also marks the Feast of Tabernacles for our preborn. It is during this time that the lungs reach their full development—ready to breathe the air or *pneumo*. "Pneumo" means air in relationship to the function of the lungs. It is at this stage, and not before, that the preborn's lungs are developed enough to house and move oxygen. The preborn's lungs are now prepared for respiration—for being filled with breath. Though most will not be born for a few more weeks, eight month old preborns are prepared as tabernacles for the Most High G-d!

Hashem blows all life and vitality into the baby to tabernacle within him at the time of his birth—igniting systems which have been prepared throughout the preborn's journey. One can actually see the infant change color from a dusky grey-blue into a beautiful rosy-pink as his first breaths or respirations are made. The Spirit (pneuma) comes to tabernacle. At approximately the same time as the Feast of Tabernacles, the lungs are ready for birth and for His Spirit.

Event 8:

9 full months
|
Feast of Dedication/Channukah:
|
|
Dedication and light--
victory over darkness!
|
Preborn Development:
|
Birth!

Chapter Nineteen: Chanukah

Parallel Events between the Journey of the Hebrews and the Journey of the Preborn: Event Eight—Birth and Dedication

Journey of the People

Channukah means dedication. It is the festival which commemorates the dedication of the Temple and it is celebrated in December—the month of Kislev. Chanukah celebrates the triumph of light over darkness, of purity over defilement, and of holiness over sin.

The story of the Festival of Lights is the story of the Maccabees. The Maccabees were a family of faithful Hebrews who prayed devoutly. They were enraged when the occupation from Assyria desecrated the Temple in Jerusalem. This one family declared war against a pagan king who occupied the land at that time—Antiochus, the king who conquered and attempted to Hellenize all of Israel. More than twenty-one centuries ago, the Holy Land was ruled by the Seleucids (Syrian-Greeks) who sought to force Israel to adopt all things Greek and Hellenize the language and culture of Israel. The King decreed that the people of Judea forsake the Law of Moses and the ancient covenants. He profaned the Holy Sabbath by killing a sow within the Holy of Holies in the Temple. This outraged the Maccabees; and against all odds, this small band of faithful Jewish men rose up to defeat one of the mightiest armies on earth. Miraculously, the Maccabees re-claimed the Holy Temple in Jerusalem and rededicated it to the worship of the one true G-d.

And thou shalt command the children of Israel that they bring thee pure oil olive beaten for the light, to cause the lamp to burn always. – Exodus 27:20

There was to be eternal light within the Temple. However, after the siege, when the priests sought to light the Temple's Holy Menorah, they could only find one cruse of pure oil which had escaped contamination by the Greeks. When they lit that one container of oil (meant for one day's supply) it supernaturally burned for eight days—just long enough for them to prepare new oil under the conditions of ritual purity. Thus, Chanukah is celebrated for eight days to commemorate this miracle.

The central activity of this festival is the nightly lighting of the Menorah, starting with a single flame on the first night, two on the second evening, and so on until the eighth night of Chanukah when all eight lights are kindled. The old story is told again on Chanukah, prayers are offered with praise and thanksgiving to G-d for "delivering the strong, into the hands of the weak; the many into the hands of the few… the wicked into the hands of the righteous".

A custom of Chanukah is to play a game with a dreidel—a spinning top—on which are inscribed the Hebrew letters *nun*, *gimmel*, *hei* and *shin*. These letters are an acronym for *Nes Gadol Hayah Sham*, "A great miracle happened there."

Journey of the Preborn

Two-hundred and eighty days have passed. Anticipation runs high. The final event is fast approaching—birth! The preborn is ready to embrace yet another change in development and life.

Preborn growth during pregnancy has been maintained in a warm (around 104 degrees F) water environment called the amniotic sac. Our preborn is about to be transformed again—born out of dark, warm water and into the open light.

Hashem has measured exactly the right amount of time it takes for each child to be ready for birth. There is a quiet time just before birth. It may be just a few days or as long as a few weeks, but in this quiet time, so much is going on. During this phase, our preborn has grown in length and weight. More brain cells mature, and a layer of brown fat has been added to the underside of his skin.

Mothers are always anxious as to when their little one will start the journey of labor and make his entrance into this world. I just tell them to be patient and wait. *The L-rd is putting on the finishing touches: stitching more hair, carefully attaching little eye lashes, speaking life into more brain cells and warming his little body with a blanket of fat.* This brown fat produces heat in order to control the baby's body temperature during and after birth. During this interval, the preborn has also been fined tuned to a greater degree. He has developed motor skills and his brain is ready to interact with a great big world. Soon, he will be born—filled with the Spirit of G-d, his temple dedicated to Him.

The preborn has been very active throughout the entire pregnancy and now during birth. During labor, he will stretch and move with each contraction, negotiating the contours of mother's womb and birth canal, opening the baby door. When the preborn engages the pelvis, plates in his skull will actually shift and overlap to reshape to the contours of his mother's body, fitting through the shape of the birth canal.

As baby descends, there is much pressure and stretching of the perineum caused by the crown of the preborn's head. Just as if this were Passover (bringing us full-circle), there is a bit of blood on the lintels of this portal. Very soon, the little face appears, rolling or rotating to one side or the other—now one shoulder, then the other. And suddenly, the labor process almost finished, our preborn comes joyfully into full view. Whoosh! Passing well beyond the confines of the uterus and birth chambers which have held them at bay, clinched ribs snap open—expanding to intake that first breath. For the first time, air passes through the vocal cords and a cry is heard. Not only is this the first time our preborn has heard his own cry, but for the first time he hears without the buffer of his mother's womb. For the first time, the preborn, now born, will feel of the pull of gravity against his limbs. For the first time, he will squint at the light, even in the dimmest birthing room.

The preborn is *changed* in a moment and is no more! Our full term preborn is suddenly changed into a newborn infant—a baby who will learn to love, live, and thrive in this new environment, continuing the covenant of Abraham. This child will continue the journey as preordained by our Creator and go on to fulfill his assignment. A perfect pregnancy, which began on Passover, has now concluded at the Festival of Lights!

It would hardly be appropriate to reach the end of our journey through gestation without sharing a celebration of birth, and I have just the one. We had just returned from a Chanukah Candle Lighting which fell on Christmas Eve. My pager went off, and it was Annie and Jim. Annie and Jim were two of the most solid Believers I had ever met, and they were in labor. Waters had broken and contractions were two to three minutes apart. This was their sixth baby, so I knew I had to get going. Grabbing my birth bag, I reassured my husband and little ones that I would be back in time to light the last of the Chanukah Candles and open presents with them.

As I arrived at Annie's, the baby was already making an entrance into the world and Jim was artfully catching. Their children, who had each been at the younger's births, were singing. They were thanking the L-rd for their new little baby and the best Christmas gift they could ever receive. Annie sang right along with them, songs of praise and thanksgiving. It seemed a choir had invaded the bedroom. The atmosphere was charged and excited, and we all heard more voices than just those that were in the room. "Must have been angels," we remarked later. A robust little boy was welcomed by his family and a chorus of angels! We cut the cord, and Jim held his still very wet son high above his head and dedicated him to Hashem as he had done with all their children.

I waited for half an hour, still no placenta. So, I asked Annie to nurse her little one again. The rich colostrum is so good for the baby and it releases oxytocin which causes contractions. But still, nothing—two hours, two and a half hours, and still no placenta. Finally, I had her stand up over a bowl and cough forcefully.

The kids thought this was hilarious, and the room was filled with peals of laughter—but it worked! The placenta was finally born, and I saw just a trickle of blood. Annie was feeling a bit tired, so she laid herself back down to sip on some chicken soup. Annie's color slowly changed to a bluish green-grey. I thought possibly she was just tired, or maybe anemic; but when I checked the pads under her, I found that she had soaked them through with blood. No more a simple trickle. My mind sped, and I began to pray.

I turned to Jim and said, "You are the priest in this home. Will you and the children pray against this hemorrhage?" Instantly, he waved to the kids to gather around. Jim told the children to sing their favorite song which was, of all things, *Victory in Jesus!* Once again, their childlike voices were joined by a heavenly choir. It was so powerful, I began to weep. Then, he laid his hands on Annie's belly; and boldly, he ordered the hemorrhage to stop releasing Annie's life. He spoke against the agents of darkness, and he ordered them to go to the throne room in Heaven where Y'shua would deal with them. He invited the Holy Spirit to intervene. We all continued to pray out loud and the entire room filled with the presence of G-d. We watched that Niagara Falls of life that was eerily leaving Annie's sweet body dry up before our very eyes. Her color returned, and before long she even wanted to get up and move around. We all gave Praise and Glory to G-d our Healer and Deliverer. It was a miracle! Oh, what a vibrant, victorious Christmas morning that was. And I made it back in time to celebrate with my family, too, just as I had promised them. The miracle of life we all saw in that room reminded me of the reason Chanukah is celebrated in the first place. Chanukah celebrates the triumph of light over darkness—and we are birthed from darkness into the light.

Feasts and Preborn Development: Eight

Mirroring Events in 280 Days

EVENT 1
Day 1
The Feast of Passover

- Hebrews **Released** from Egypt on the 14th day of the month of Nisan (release from sin)
- **Release** of the ova on the 14th day of the woman's cycle.

EVENT 2
Day 2
The Feast of Unleavened Bread

- **No leaven** in homes (dying to self)
- Two become one as the ova is fertilized in a pure, leaven **free** environment.

EVENT 3
Day 4
The Feast of First Fruits

- **Wave offering** to the L-rd (celebration of new life)
- The zygote is moved through the fallopian tube **in a distinct waving motion** by hair-like cilia/fimbria. This is a 4 day process.

EVENT 4
50 Days Later
The Feast of Shavuot

- The people were given **a new identity** as a nation and Bride!
- The embryo is scientifically recognizable as a human being (called a fetus) and is given **a new identity.**

Feasts and Preborn Development: Eight

Mirroring Events in 280 Days

EVENT 5
7 Months
The Feast of Trumpets (Rosh Hashanah)

- **Trumpets are blown** calling the people to answer and to repent
- The preborn's **hearing develops** and he can now hear and distinguish sounds from inside the womb.

EVENT 6
7.5 Months (10 Days Later)
Yom Kippur (Day of Atonement)

- A blood sacrifice is required as **there is life within the blood**.
- The preborn now has a new component in his blood called Hemoglobin-A. **There is now life within his blood**.

EVENT 7
Just Before the 8th Month
The Feast of Tabernacles

- **Hashem tabernacled with His people** in the wilderness.
- The preborn's lungs are now ready to receive and move air. He has been prepared as a tabernacle for the Spirit of G-d.

EVENT 8
9 Full Months
Feast of Dedications (Chanukah)

- Chanukah is about new beginnings— **dedication and light**.
- The once preborn is now **born into the light and dedicated to G-d**!

Chapter Twenty: A Third Journey: The Journey of the Bride

The Bride of the Lamb is not mentioned by name in the Torah, but we find her in the Prophets [Isaiah 54:5, Jeremiah 3:20, Jeremiah 31:32]. We also find her in Revelations.

"Come hither, I will shew thee the Bride, the Lamb's wife" – Revelations 21:9

From Sinai, Hashem has groomed Israel as His wife. Through Abraham's bloodline, He conceived a son—our Messiah. Now, G-d seeks a pure and faithful Bride for His Son.

Let's rewind back to our opening wedding scene. Do you recall that night after the betrothal when the groom left to go build a home for the bride? It would be a year or so before he returned to claim his bride, and not until his father said it was time. When the Father gives permission, the Son will come for His Bride. He will come, like Hebrew grooms always come, in the middle of the night.

Believers the world over have been waiting and longing since Y'shua left. They are waiting for the Bridegroom to come for them—His Bride. This is one of the great mysteries of the New Testament and is the promise Y'shua made to the first century Believers. He promised that He would come again to receive a pure people to Himself.

"And if I go and prepare a place for you, I will come again, and receive you unto Myself; that where I am, there ye may be also" –John 14:3.

"And every man that hath this hope in Him purifies himself, even as He is pure" –1 John 3:3.

As the Son waits for His Father's command, He beseeches Believers to remain sanctified and faithful in their waiting. The very thought of His coming, and of the home He is now preparing, ought to be enough to encourage us to Holy Living. Have we escaped the wiles of the enemy of G-d? Have we run to Him and not to the counterfeits? Do we need to go around the mountain again?

As she waits, just as the brides of ancient Israel waited, the Bride prepares for her Bridegroom nightly. She knows He will come for her with a shout and the blast of a trumpet. She does not know when He is coming, but she knows when the time is close. If we are not ignorant of these things, His coming will not surprise us.

But ye, brethren, are not in darkness, that that day should overtake you as a thief. —1 Thessalonians 5:4

Just as a bride faithfully waits for the return of her bridegroom, we should not grow weary in waiting or lose our joy as so many do. Joyfully, we must continue to watch and stay awake. The Bridegroom is about to arrive!

Looking at the chart in the following section, I ask you—are we approaching that final hour? Is our time of waiting almost over? Will the great trump soon sound? When the great trump sounds, the miracle of all miracles will take place. Believers will rise from the earth, the graves will give up their dead, and all Believers will be changed and outfitted for *immortality in a moment.*

> *For the L-rd himself shall descend from heaven with a shout, with the voice of the archangel, and with the trump of G-d; and the dead in Christ shall rise first: 17. Then we, which are alive and remain, shall be caught up together with them in the clouds, to meet the L-rd in the air: and so shall we ever be with the L-rd.*
> *—1 Thessalonians 4:16-17*

So where are we on the time-line? At what stage are we in this journey? Y'shua died on Passover, at the exact time the lambs were slain. He was buried on the first day of Unleavened Bread, and He rose as the First Fruits of the resurrection in which we hope. He established His covenant with Israel on Shavuot and renewed that same covenant on a Shavuot (Pentecost) many years later. We now wait for the Feast of Trumpets. But how long until the trumpet sounds? Do we have ears to hear?

> *"Be careful, keep calm, and don't be afraid. Do not lose heart ... If you do not stand firm in your faith, you will not stand at all." – Isaiah 7:4, 9*

The return of the children of Israel to the Promised Land, the ingathering of all those who worship the L-rd, is taking place right now! The Bridegroom will come to collect His Bride when the time has come, when she has been proven faithful. Are we ready?

The true Church, the Bride of Christ, all Believers—all of Israel and the stranger who has been grafted in—will be in that company when our Bridegroom comes to catch us up. If all humankind possesses the imprint of every feast written in the Torah, then all people have the chance to choose life as the Bride of Y'shua.

In the introduction, we talked about a wedding. Then, we explored the journey of the Chosen people and the journey of the preborn. This journey is the journey of all mankind, and so it is also the journey of His Bride. We that love Him are betrothed to Him. We should seek to know Him fully, and to never miss an appointment with Him. It is my hope that in reading what I've written here, you have become more knowledgeable about the events of the Torah Feasts and about the relevance of these events to all of our lives.

The Feasts and the Journey of the Bride: Eight Mirroring Events in 280 Days

EVENT 1
Day 1
The Feast of Passover

- Hebrews **Released** from Egypt on the 14th day of the month of Nisan (release from sin)
- Y'shua died on the 14th day. We were **released** from sin.

EVENT 2
Day 2
The Feast of Unleavened Bread

- **No leaven** in homes (dying to self)
- Y'shua buried.

EVENT 3
Day 3
The Feast of First Fruits

- **Wave offering** to the L-rd (celebration of new life)
- Y'shua resurrected as the first fruits of salvation.

EVENT 4
50 Days Later
The Feast of Shavuot

- The people were given **a new identity** as a nation and Bride!
- Believers received the Holy Spirit and received a new identity as the Church.

Y'shua fulfilled at His first coming

The Feasts and the Journey of the Bride: Eight Mirroring Events in 280 Days

EVENT 5
7 Months
The Feast of Trumpets (Rosh Hashanah)
- **Trumpets are blown** calling the people to answer and to repent
- The Bride is called up with the blast of a trumpet.

EVENT 6
7.5 Months (10 Days Later)
Yom Kippur (Day of Atonement)
- A blood sacrifice is required as **there is life within the blood**.
- Atoned by His blood.

EVENT 7
Just Before the 8th Month
The Feast of Tabernacles
- **Hashem tabernacled with His people** in the wilderness.
- Y'shua tabernacles with His people for 1000 years.

EVENT 8
9 Full Months
Feast of Dedications (Chanukah)
- Chanukah is about new beginnings - **dedication and light**.
- The dedication of eternity.

Y'shua will fulfill at His second coming

Conclusion

A timeline is being played out right before our eyes! We can see the blue-print of life that G-d spoke into being, which resides deep within the memory of our cells. We have experienced pre-birth meetings with Holy G-d and now have a new understanding of these meetings through The Feasts. As we come to understand this as reality and begin thinking like a Hebrew, the journey, our journey, becomes clearer.

With conscious awareness of The Feasts comes renewed hope. We know we are on a journey. We know G-d will honor His contract with us. We know we will be changed in a moment and will meet our King in the air!

Each of us has experienced every single one of The Feasts in utero, by design of our Creator. These appointments with G-d have been imprinted into our spirit, regardless of our race or creed. This is a beautiful hand engraved wedding invitation. *Everyone* is invited.

Have you accepted that invitation? Have you accepted the Jewish Y'shua, the son of G-d, as your L-rd and Savior? Is He your Bridegroom? Are you faithfully awaiting His return?

With all that said, would you please excuse me? I must finish getting ready for the wedding of all weddings. You have your invitation, and I do hope you will come with me, where Everything Old is New Again!

Study References

Husband-Coached Childbirth
    Robert A. Bradley, MD, OBGYN
Glory Zone
    David and Stephanie Herzog
    ISBN 10:0-7684-2434-8
King James Bible
New International
New King James
    Version of the Bible/Dakes Annotated
Message Bible
Torah
Expecting Miracles: Finding Meaning an Spiritually in Pregnancy through Judaism
    Chana Weisberg
    ISBN 965-7108-5109
    Israel
Confessions of a Medical Heretic
Dr. Robert S. Mendelsohn, M.D.
    Contemporary Books 1979
    4255 West Toughy Avenue
    Chicago, Ill 60646-1975 USA
Walid Shoebat
    G-d's War on Terrorism
English Hebrew Bilingual Dictionary Transliterated
    Prolog Publishing House POB 300 Rosh Ha'ayin, 48101
    Israel
Living Judaism Today
    Ari L. Goldman
    Simon and Shuster

EVENT 1	EVENT 2	EVENT 3	EVENT 4
Day 1	Day 2	Day 4	50 Days Later
The Feast of Passover Hebrews **Released** from Egypt on the 14th day of the month of Nisan (release from sin)	The Feast of Unleavened Bread **No leaven** in homes (dying to self)	The Feast of First Fruits **Wave offering** to the L-rd—Celebration of new life!	The Feast of Shavuot The people were given a **new identity** as a nation and Bride!
Release of the ova on the 14th day of the woman's cycle	Two become one as the ova is fertilized in a pure, **leaven free** environment	The zygote is moved through the fallopian **tube in a distinct waving motion** by hair-like ilia/fimbria. This is a 4 day Process.	The embryo is scientifically recognizable as a human being (called a fetus) and is given **a new identity**.
Release from sin— Y'shua died	Y'shua buried	Y'shua resurrected as the first fruits of salvation	Believers received the Holy Spirit and received a new identity as the Church

EVENT 5	EVENT 6	EVENT 7	EVENT 8
7 Months	7 ½ Months	Almost 8 Mo.	9 Full Mo.
The Feast of Trumpets (Rosh Hashanah) **Trumpets are blown** calling the people to answer and to repent	Yom Kippur (Day of Atonement) A blood sacrifice is required as **there is life within the blood.**	The Feast of Tabernacles **Hashem tabernacled with His people** in the wilderness.	Feast of Dedications (Chanukah) Chanukah is about new beginnings **dedication and light**.
The preborn's **hearing develops** and he can now hear and distinguish sounds from inside the womb.	The preborn now has a new component in his blood called Hemoglobin-A. **There is now life within his blood.**	The preborn's lungs are now ready to receive and move air. He has been prepared as a tabernacle for the Spirit of G-d.	The once preborn is now **born into the light and dedicated to G-d**!
The Bride is called up with the blast of a trumpet	Atoned by His blood	Y'shua tabernacles with His people for 1000 years	The dedication of eternity

Made in the USA
Lexington, KY
06 April 2013